REMEMBER WHEN

A business success story, built on family

Norma Kier
with Rhonda Lauritzen

Like Rain Publishing ◆ Utah, 84412
Produced by Evalogue.Life

Like Rain Publishing
221 N. Washington Blvd. #13922
Ogden, UT 84412

Produced by Evalogue.Life – Tell Your Story!

Evalogue.Life

www.Evalogue.Life

Printed in the United States of America
First printing 2018

DEDICATIONS

This book is written in loving memory of my wonderful husband Jim who gave me so much love. Together we had a very busy, exciting, and rewarding life. Also in honor of our five incredible children, 20 grandchildren, 10 great-grandchildren, and counting.

To my brother Jon and sister Barb, you helped shaped me into who I am and I love you dearly.

The proceeds from the sale of *Remember When* will go to Lymphoma Cancer in loving memory of James E. Kier.

ACKNOWLEDGMENTS

I love and appreciate more friends, employees, colleagues and subcontractors than we can count. You have become our extended family. We mentioned many of you by name, but I worry about anyone I may have missed. You all made a difference in our lives and I sincerely apologize if anyone was left out.

In that spirit, we made the difficult decision to not list our grandchildren by name in the body of this book. That many names would be confusing to the reader and I would never want placement to appear as though favoring anyone.

We acknowledge the many individuals who helped provide oral history, research, and editing for this book. We made every attempt to get the details right, although memories can fail and in the case of families there will always be different versions of the truth depending on where one sits.

1951

BRITANNIA

It all started the night of the accident. If I knew then what I know now, would I still have gone out? Would I have changed anything? Perhaps I might have left my new earrings safe in their little box or maybe I would have dallied another thirty seconds. I think not, though. Even knowing about a coma and a long recovery, I would still do it all the same way, right down to the outfit and the earrings. I would trace my footsteps and pace the clock. The accident was worth it, not because of where I woke up—in a hospital—but because of where I wound up. The worst of luck in a split second altered the trajectory of my life and who I would become. Blind chance for me, but instinctive action by an athletic young man named Jim Kier.

It was January 6, 1951, on the outskirts of Ottawa, and I rubbed at the windowpane to gauge the blizzard. My friends Joan and Liz would knock soon so we could walk to the Friday night dance together. Darkness already pooled on snow-thick streets, but that sort of nonsense does not keep Canadian fifteen-year-olds from a social life, especially during winter when everybody needs a boost.

They arrived in coats and boots, but came inside long enough to compare outfits. I had on a skirt and a pretty sweater that my mum had knitted and I showed them new football earrings my parents had given me for Christmas. Mum looked pleased that I admired them with my friends.

I zipped up a pea-green coat that I didn't especially love and wrapped on a luxurious knitted scarf from my mum's mum. We called her Granny. There was absolutely nothing better than those paper-wrapped packages that came shipped to us. My siblings and I would run our fingers over the creases and anticipate the beautiful things we always found inside.

After I was bundled, we three girlfriends clomped outside together. While we trudged to the school, steamy puffs of breath fogged the air and I squinted my eyes to keep a flurry of flakes from melting my vision.

That was the last memory I retained from that night. After I awoke in the hospital, others had to repeat later details to me through a swampiness and white-light pounding in my head. Aside from the concussion and bruising everywhere, it took time to grasp that I was lucky to have a beating heart.

As it was told to me, we walked through the little park where streetcars and horse-drawn sleighs turned around, and then a half-mile or so to the elementary school. Across from the school, I stood between Joan and Liz at the intersection. Hats covered our ears and thick snow muffled all sound, while our vision was limited to a few feet. We did not hear the car coming, nor could we have known that the young man driving it had been drinking. I stepped into what I thought was a clear street at the same moment the big car flew onto our scene, driving too recklessly even if it had been a dry urban street. My friends lagged a step behind—enough to spare them. As the car crashed into me, their shrieks were absorbed by the whiteout. My ninety-pound body hurtled eighty-five feet and landed in a massive snowdrift. The blow, of course, left me unconscious. The force of it took my earrings and we never did find them. My coat ripped all the way up the back.

Joan and Liz raced to the school and ran so fast through both sets of doors that a cold shaft of air hit kids and adults milling about in the lobby. People whipped around midsentence as the girls' halting words pierced through pleasantries. "A car…Norma's been hit!" They pointed across the street.

An adult chaperone ran and placed his arms on Liz's shoulders. "How bad?" he asked. Adrenaline coursed through Liz, making her tongue stick on simple words. The blood drained from my friends' faces as mine certainly had. How could they describe seeing their friend fly through the air? Their pale immobility must have spoken fear in place of sentences. Some teachers and older boys charged outside while a woman telephoned an ambulance.

They found my body crumpled and sunken into deep snow. A teacher brushed frozen wisps from my face and checked my breathing. It was shallow and uneven, but still there.

"Norma. Norma." They patted my cheeks so I would come to.

"Don't move her," the teacher said. "She could have a spinal injury."

They pulled up my eyelids to see if my eyes were responsive and checked for bleeding or broken bones through bulky layers. Someone held an umbrella over me and they heaped more coats on, trying to keep my unresponsive frame warm. They waited, shifting and shivering.

One of the older boys was a summer lifeguard, very athletic, and sprang into action. He had been among the first to reach me and although he probably stood aside for the adults, he shifted his weight, checking his watch every few seconds and keeping his muscles ready to move at a nod. Others gathered in rings, huddling together in a helpless murmur. One minute. Ten. Too many minutes passed and the group anxiously discussed what to do. I was growing colder, so they motioned to a chaperone who had pulled his car up, idling in case it was needed. A teacher pointed at the athletic teenager, calling him to action at last. Jimmy Kier knelt down, burrowed his strong arms underneath and scooped my body from the snow. He picked his way through parting onlookers and with every step, his arms pillowed my body against jostling. He crouched and held his breath while placing me into the back seat. His heart clenched as he glanced once more at the small girl in the car. He had noticed me as one of the younger girls in a big crowd that went around together, but we had not really become acquainted. Now I looked pixie-like and pale in the back seat. He gently pushed the door shut and the car immediately fishtailed and sped away, driven by an expert in snow.

"She's just a girl," Jim pleaded with God under his breath as he watched the car disappear into the night. "Please don't let her die."

My mum got the nightmare call alone since Dad was on Army assignment elsewhere as a Chief Warrant Officer in the Royal Canadian Engineers. Someone drove Mum to the hospital while I lay there asleep and unable to speak. I would have reminded her how strong I was, all the pushups Dad had me do, and how I made basketball captain that year. I couldn't tell her any of that, though. She paced on squeaky floors for eighteen terrifying hours of my coma, unable to rest in case I awoke or worse, didn't. She must have bargained with God to not let her eldest die, second-guessing the decision to let me go to the dance and thinking, "I shouldn't have let her out in a blizzard. Her dad would have said no, she is too young. Norma does so much for me and her siblings. I know her heart. I will do anything you ask of me and anything for her. Just name the sacrifice, God. I'm yours, please just don't take her."

I finally awoke confused and unaware of raccoon-black eyes, which sounds cuter than it was. I grimaced when I finally saw myself in the mirror because that made it all very real.

After the doctors said I was on the road to full recovery, Mum had to go back home to take care of the other kids, so I was quite happy when the doctor cleared me for visitors and two boys from school, Jimmy Kier and Freddie Goodfellow, came to see me. We knew of each other, but I was only a freshman and they were grade 13 and we hadn't talked much before then.

I must say it is a strange feeling to wake up and realize that a lot has happened while you have been asleep. People have appeared in your life and seem to know a lot about you without you knowing why. The boys had been calling since the accident and they explained to me how Jimmy had put me in the car. Jimmy flicked a shock of jet-black hair that had fallen into hazel eyes and said, "We've been worried sick about you." I blushed at the idea of him picking me up, and then I thought of my black eyes and became more self-conscious. It was bad enough for Mum to see me like that, but much worse when it's two of the older boys from school. I touched my face, wanting to hide behind my hands. Then Jimmy said, "Aw, you look fine." I shook my head knowing he was lying, but it was nice of him to say it.

We made small talk and while they were there, I asked something. "Do you know what happened to my earrings?" They shook their heads and said, "Haven't seen them. They must have been lost in the accident." I tried to hold back, but the more I tried the more the tears began to spill from my eyes. I was mad at myself for being unable to control my emotions and especially in front of them. I did not realize how off-kilter I

8

still was; I could only think about how much I loved those earrings and how unfair it was to lose them after only 11 days.

A nurse came in and decided that the boys should go since I needed rest. They asked if they could come back and the nurse looked in my direction. I must have seemed expectant at the idea of visitors and she said, "Of course you may."

This cheered me up because I had no other prospects for visits. The trek was too long for Mum via streetcar and she rarely had a penny to spare in the best of circumstances. Now there would be expenses because of this. Also, when you're military, you don't have family around to take the other children. It occurred to me then that a group of Army wives must have rallied around her when this happened. Mum always had a lot of friends wherever we moved. She had English sensibilities and put on a brave face, producing meals and doing men's haircuts at a dollar each. Her fortitude now reminded me of the years our little family had spent at Shawnigan Lake on Vancouver Island while Dad was in World War II in Europe. It must have been a harrowing time for Mum, but this period was bright with happy memories for me.

I drifted to sleep and the next day awoke in a nostalgic mood. I pulled out the scrapbook my mum had brought, paging to a photograph of our white clapboard home at Shawnigan Lake. I had labeled it "Shangri La." In a hospital bed with a pounding head, I had nothing to do but replay memories of how we kids would dive off the boat dock into chilly waters nearly every day. We caught crawfish and followed the railroad tracks that curved along the lakeshore behind our home. We ran free in the thick woods and practically lived in the water and on the pebbled beach. A child never knows boredom in a place like that.

As a child, I read the Encyclopedia and the Book of Knowledge so I could play teacher with my siblings. My brother Jon was a naturally precocious boy who learned to read before entering First Grade, and later skipped two grades. When people remarked how smart he was, he would tell them, "Norma taught me to read." Jon would enter the University of Alberta at age 15. Next came my sister Barb who was always my partner in crime and in pictures it was hard to tell the two of us apart. Our youngest brother Bob had many physical difficulties since birth, which made life even harder on Mum.

Granny often lived with us during our childhood. She had twin girls, my mum and aunt, before my grandfather passed away, and she never remarried. Granny was an absolute delight in our lives and gave me many lessons in fortitude. I once came home in the dumps after being picked on for being small. She said, "Always remember. Dynamite comes in small packages."

In the middle of war, goods were scarce, but Mum and Granny's British stoicism nipped any complaining in the bud. "Think of our relatives in England. We are safe on this beautiful lake, and we have plenty. We must pray for them and for Dad." Aside from praying, Mum kept us from the harrowing details of Dad's service. Perhaps she did not know herself. Later he ran an office, but in the war, he led troops through minefields to disarm them. He was very, very lucky to not receive physical injuries or be killed.

Mum and Granny held our happiness together with knitting, embroidery, and games of Cribbage. A soldier's pay was always meager, but Mum's resourcefulness was remarkable. With Dad overseas, his paychecks went to her, which gave her more control over our family's finances. Even with rationing, I do not recall wanting for anything. These were hallmarks of her generation. When the men came home bearing silent burdens and fighting dead enemies, nobody would ever be the same. Mum made do.

Lying in bed alone, feelings of nostalgia turned into longing, and I missed my handsome dad. He could be difficult, but I loved him, and the two of us spent a lot of time together. All the kids relished it when Dad took us to swim in the lake while he read under a tree. He and I shared a name—Norman and Norma—and he gave each of the four children a nickname. Mine had been "Duchess" until once in school I spotted a picture of a Duchess in a history book. She was old and had a double chin so I came home and said, "I don't want to be Duchess anymore." After that it was shortened to "Dutch," which kids at Nepean High School still called me. Dad and I also shared a love of sports and Dad would sometimes take me to a bar to watch a game. He tried to show off my athletic abilities, which embarrassed me.

I did not like attention, so it was okay that I would not receive a lot of visitors in the hospital, especially with how I looked. Since Jimmy

Kier and Freddie Goodfellow had already broken the ice, though, I was eager for their next visit. They showed up in the middle of the school day so I asked, "Shouldn't you be in class?"

Freddie gave a devil-may-care shrug. He'd ditch school on a whim, but Jim broke into a grin that seemed half business and half mischief. His eyes twinkled, "I will tell them you need someone to bring your homework." They had no intention of burdening me with lessons, but an excuse is an excuse. They brought a radio instead, and I spent my time alone listening to music.

One day, Jimmy arrived by himself, looking handsome in a leather bomber jacket. He had an athletic build and always looked nice with shoes shined. The clothes underneath his weathered jacket were ironed crisp, a task he did himself each night. His reckless hair and half-grin were casual, and he was always swooping back thick hair so dark it almost looked blue in the hospital light. He placed a little white box on the food tray beside me.

"What's this?" I asked.

"Open it," he said.

I lifted the top and perched on fluffy cotton was a pair of football earrings, an exact match to the ones I lost.

"We went looking around the school, but you got hit pretty hard. Come spring, some kid might find one in the dirt, but the odds of recovering a pair are about nil."

I flushed and asked, "Did you buy these?"

He shrugged and said, "I have a job."

I was touched and said, "That is very, very thoughtful, Jimmy. Thank you." He seemed happy.

The day before they let me go home, I said to Jimmy, "I'm getting out tomorrow, so I guess you don't have to come any more."

Jimmy looked wounded, so I added, "Unless you want to."

At that, he recovered and said, "With you missing school, I thought I could bring your lessons and help you catch up. I've had your classes." What a nice boy. He was smart and could be a great help. I nodded and it was settled.

He came to visit me at our modest little house. Whenever someone new comes, you see your place through their eyes. I had nothing to be embarrassed about and our home was clean, if not much to look at. There was always a smell of shampoo from Mum's make-do beautician salon, and there was laughter and chit-chat from other Army wives. I envied the easy way Mum had with people and how she seemed to effortlessly establish a new clientele with each move. The odors of hair tonics—which always seemed cheerful to me—would blend with whatever Mum might be cooking that day. It was always tasty and satisfying. From her, I learned the art of coming up with a good meal; she could do it with practically nothing.

Although we lived on the outskirts of the nation's capital and our town of Britannia was a good-sized suburb, some of the homes like ours did not have indoor plumbing. This meant every drop of water inside had to be pumped out back and brought in. For bath time, Mum warmed water in a kettle and put it into a big metal washtub. The habit in households at the time was that the dad would bathe first, then Mum, and on down to the youngest child (don't throw the baby out with the bath water!). Mum would add more warm water throughout. She also got up early every morning when the house was icy cold to start the coal stove. Heat would gradually rise into the upstairs where Barb and I slept, often together for warmth. Before bedtime, Mum draped our pajamas over the stove for that momentary pleasure of heat before dashing upstairs into the covers. On washday in the winter, she hung our clothes outside and had to bring them in frozen, standing everything against the wall like stiff gingerbread men. Dad's long johns made us laugh.

We used an outhouse, situated inside a shed out back. Every six months, my brother and I had the job of pasting pictures from the magazine section of the Saturday newspaper onto the outhouse walls. This was a typical setup, and with such bitter winters, everyone had a pot under the bed for evening use. It was so cold we would run like mad from the outhouse back inside again, and Dad played a game to see if we could race in before the outhouse door clapped shut.

Now Jimmy entered the living room, greeted my mum and said, "You have a nice home." She offered a bright smile and looked over instructions from my teachers.

"Start off light," she said. "The doctor said we mustn't push her." My head still felt too fuzzy for subjects like math, but we thought I might try typing. After the war, career choices for unmarried women included teaching, nursing, or secretarial work. I showed an interest in "commercial subjects" like bookkeeping and shorthand, so during my freshman year I had signed up for typing.

We plunked out a few lines, but spent the rest of our time visiting. I wasn't so chatty unless I knew someone well, but Jimmy put me at ease saying, "You can call me Jim," which I did from then on. He was quite a storyteller and when he got started with a joke, his whole body shook and tears welled up in his eyes. He drew me into whatever he described, the many jobs he already held, funny stories like getting covered with mustard at a hot dog stand where he worked, or his goal of building a life someday. Perhaps he would be a doctor or maybe a history teacher. Now that we were getting better acquainted, he could get me talking too—about sports or whatever else. Regardless of the topic, the conversation flowed easily.

Jim was casual in the way he talked about the family with whom he lived, and he liked them. He never mentioned his own mother who I gathered was alive but just *elsewhere*. There was no hint of a father, and I sensed it best not to pry. He had lived with his Scottish grandmother nearby until her health failed and she had to move in with his Aunt Jean and Uncle Jack in Toronto. He confessed that he tried to stay in his grandmother's home for a while by himself, but the authorities caught on and arranged for a family in town to take him in. He radiated a special devotion when he spoke of his grandmother, tinged with the sorrow of deep loneliness for her. She passed away in Toronto when he was just 14.

Jim came to help me every afternoon that month until I went back to school. I was flattered that this very handsome older boy had taken an interest in little me. I remembered how some of my girlfriends watched him lifeguarding at Britannia Pier, a lively beach where all the teenagers spent summer days. Jimmy Kier had been the object of more than one crush by the bevvy of girls in our big circle of friends we called "The Gang." Maybe thirty of us teenagers would congregate at the pier or in Britannia Park by our home. It was such a fun bunch of kids that could find amusement in any season. Everyone had a nickname and we all sized-up potential pairings among the opposite sex. The kids picked up on my nickname "Dutch" and Jim was "Jimmy." Among the group was Freddie Goodfellow and the Dooher teenagers who were part of a big Catholic family. Betty Dooher was a popular girl, good at everything, and a ringleader of sorts in our group. She was a friend of mine, and Jim was friends with her older brothers, including Mike who was already a pilot in the Canadian Air Force. We all spent a lot of time in the Dooher home. Now Jim was a regular at my home, too, drawn to family life and our mothers' excellent cooking.

When I had recovered enough, one of my first outings was a short walk with Jim, and I was chipper on several accounts. I was excited to wear my new Navy blue coat. Mum had taken me shopping after the ugly pea green one got ruined in the accident. I tried not to act pleased it was ruined because my parents worked so hard for every penny, but I couldn't help enjoying a bit of good fortune out of the deal. I did not often get to choose something so nice. I was also glad for some fresh air and I had come to look forward to Jim's visits. My siblings had begun teasing me when I flitted about the house.

We strolled through Britannia Park, a picturesque spot. In the winter, big sleighs carrying twenty or thirty people turned around in the park. During nice weather, it was an amusement park and many of the teenagers had summer jobs there.

As we moseyed along, Jim dug both hands into his pockets and cleared his throat, "Norma, can I take you on a real date?" My stomach fluttered and that's how our official courtship began.

For our date, we cut out of school early and I grabbed my things from the locker. As we sat on the streetcar to a movie, I looked down at my feet and blushed. I was mortified to notice that I was wearing one of my own boots, and the other from my locker mate: one black and one brown. I didn't say anything, just hoping Jim would not notice, but I was in luck. Jim Kier was forever oblivious to mismatched boots.

For my first semi-formal school dance, I did not have a nice enough dress to wear, so Mum sent me shopping with ten dollars and my siblings in tow. Mum earned every bit of extra spending money for our family from haircuts. She was always generous with me, and seemed especially tender since my accident. In the dress shop, I fell in love with the prettiest white eyelet dress, but my heart sank at the fifteen-dollar price tag. An extra five dollars meant five more haircuts. We kids had an insatiable appetite for coats, hats, and gloves so I knew how frivolous such a lovely dress was, especially since Mum knitted or sewed most of our clothes. I ran the textured fabric through my fingertips and circled the shop in hopes of finding something less expensive, biting my lip every time I returned to this one. I decided to call Mum. I have always remembered how sweet she was to grant me this luxury. She had so little for herself, but when we were happy, her eyes sparkled like sunlight on the lake.

Jim and I were becoming a pair, although Freddie Goodfellow and others were generally around, too. I got a kick out of how Freddie, President of the Junior Achievement Club, enjoyed baiting Jim in debates about politics or world affairs saying, "You work too hard, my friend. We've got to live while we are young."

Even at that age, Jim stated his ambitions, "I intend to make something of myself. I will build a life with my bare hands if I have to."

Freddie volleyed his opinions back, "Look at the state of the world, Jim. Nothing lasts."

Jim warned, "Freddie, live like that and *you* won't last."

I liked the banter and admired them both. Jim and Freddie were each handsome, but in different ways and with their looks almost juxtaposed to their personalities. Freddie had fine features and fair skin, but daredevil inclinations. Jim's muscular build and wild black hair gave him an intense look, yet he had the softer manners and more jovial nature.

That spring I had to testify against the 18-year-old fellow who hit me with his car that night. I was sick at having to speak, but I had been officially summoned and felt grateful that my Dad and Mum were both there to support me. Attention made me so nervous, I was almost glad the accident had left me unconscious with no awareness of people standing around looking at me.

In school, I tried to escape notice by being average. I would rather have the worst stomach flu than deliver an assignment in front of the class. In the first grade, I had to recite a simple speech and got myself physically sick from nerves. I tried to stay home, but my parents weren't having it, telling me I was making it worse in my imagination. Well, it was just as bad in real life. Standing in front of everyone, I willed for a giant hole to swallow me. Without athletics, I could not imagine making friends each time we moved.

I would do my best testifying, however, because it was very important that this young man pay my medical bills. That pressure heightened my anxiety, which worsened when I entered and saw the walls lined with Mounties in imposing red uniforms. My vision went blurry, my mouth was cotton, and the room became deadly quiet except for feverish clicking by a court reporter. When counsel asked a question, I spoke, but the Judge had to interrupt, "Speak up, miss." I started again, searching hard for my voice. I answered the question, and then another until it was finished. Then I walked wobbly-kneed back to my seat. I did not faint.

We waited for the proceedings to finish and I agonized over what I had said, wondering if my performance had been enough. The verdict came back and the young man was ordered to pay our bills. I breathed again.

I walked out with my dad and felt triumphant. The young man who had just been sentenced spotted me and sauntered up. He had a cocky air and said, "So can I drive you home?"

Dad growled at him, "You get out of here!" The young man just laughed. Some nerve after having run me down.

Now the snow was starting to melt and the first crocuses peeked out. One afternoon, I came running through the door as Mum was giving a haircut to a young boy in the kitchen. The boy played with something in his lap that he had retrieved from a yellow box of toys she always brought out for children. I went for my room, but Mum called after me.

"Norma, we have news." It already sounded like an apology and I hesitated before turning around.

"Your dad has been transferred. We are moving this summer."

I felt kicked into a wall. I had taken moves in stride before because that was the lot of a military family. Somehow in Britannia, though, I had been lulled into a sense of permanency. My life was going well. I had friends. I belonged. There were fun things to do. I liked our school. There was Jim.

Mum continued. "The new posting is Wainwright, Alberta."

I had never heard of it so I ran upstairs and yanked out a map. Wainwright was two thousand miles away and there was a big blank space surrounding the dot marking its location. The closest real city was Edmonton, nearly two hundred miles away. There would be no visiting.

Wainwright might as well be Africa. I collapsed into a heap of tears. The unfairness was devastating. I cried for days and confided the news to Jim. He listened and his shoulders sank, hangdog.

"I don't know how I could lose you, Norma," he said. In those words, I understood how much had already been taken from him by age 19. Right then, I hated the Army with every muscle in my body and I was angry at my parents for choosing military life. I resented that as soon as I found my groove, orders yanked me out by the roots. You might think it would get easier, and maybe it did for some people, but each time I moved, I wilted like a tender plant, dug up in the wrong season and plunked into inhospitable dirt. Wainwright would certainly be the wrong place for me, a Podunk outpost, far away from friends. Would they remember me? Would Jim move on to someone else?

No, I thought to myself. *He is the loyal type, too. He is.*

Jim looked at me and squared his shoulders. I could see his mind looking for solutions. He said, "Maybe your folks will let you remain here. Families would let you stay with them. I should know." I fanaticized about that for a while, but I also knew my protective father. He would not hear of it, and while Mum had sympathy, she would keep our family together. My sentence had been decreed, and I already understood there would be no appeal.

Jim said, "We'll figure something out," and he added with a wry smile, "We could run away together." *Maybe we should*, I thought.

Winter inched into spring and Britannia Pier, where Jim worked, opened for the season. Outside school, Jim and I spent every minute we could together. A sense of immediacy painted our time with richer color. Most teenagers walk around thinking the world will continue on forever, but ours had an end date. Dad had announced that date, and I was dumbstruck at this final insult: my sixteenth birthday would be our last day. Some sweet sixteen.

I hardly spoke for the better part of a week and everyone stayed out of my way until Dad got sharp, "Buck up or else, young lady." I stomped off, but got in line. He meant business.

The weeks leading to our departure enveloped us with the type of longing that makes every moment bittersweet. My parents let me spend every evening with Jim and the simplest activities like buying watermelon or walking in the rain felt special. So many emotions filled me that at first light each morning, my eyes came open with excitement at the prospect of seeing Jim. Later I remembered the awful dread that we were another day closer to my birthday. Jim and I schemed, but there were flaws in each plan. Jim kept saying, "I'll think of something."

Neither denial nor scheming prevented the time from passing. Dad got our train tickets and at exactly 11:59 p.m. on my sixteenth birthday, a locomotive would charge into town and stop long enough to rip me away with my hands grasping at the city's lights.

The day before departure, Betty Dooher threw me a going away party, which was very, very nice of her. Jim walked me home, and we lay in the grass looking for the North Star. We named Polaris "our star," and all around us magical fireflies glowed.

On July the third, the best I could do was memorize every detail about Jim. Since it was my birthday, I got to choose the activity, and on a clear summer evening I wanted to go on a double date at the drive-in. Jim and I chose the loveseats—wooden benches two people wide—at the front. I leaned in and we cuddled in the dark. I breathed in his smell and tried to make the clock stop. This was home. What would we do?

Afterward, Freddie drove me to the station. Jim and I sat in the back seat and he took my hand. Then he looked at me with intense resolve, like he had finally figured out the plan. My heart pounded at his words.

"I'm crazy about you. These last months have been the happiest of my life." I listened. "We're too young, but as soon as we can, I want to marry you and I will work three jobs to make it happen. I will prove that I am good enough, if you will have me."

He stopped and waited for an answer. I gazed back at him and with a pounding heart said, "Yes. I want this."

He looked as though a mountain of pressure had been relieved. This was our answer. We could wait it out now. He said, "This will have to be our secret because your dad would come unglued. Someday I will propose right with a ring, but I couldn't let you get on that train without knowing if you would be mine."

I said to him, "I am yours."

For the first time since I heard we were leaving, I felt at peace. Jim had given me quite a sixteenth birthday gift. Then I had to go.

1951 – 1957

ALBERTA

———◆———

Jim saw me off at the station and I boarded through sobs. We got settled and through blurred tears in my eyes, I watched the city fade into a black Ontario night. My whole body heaved. Dad patted me on the arm and said, "You'll be alright. Time heals everything, especially puppy love." I couldn't even look at him. This was not puppy love. They never knew I became engaged on the very day I turned sixteen. We weren't just silly kids. We knew something true.

I must have finally fallen asleep to the train's rhythm and awoke to wide prairie landscapes. At first consciousness, I felt a strange duality: I tingled with excitement that I was engaged, and felt deep sadness that my *fiancé* –I turned the word over in my mind—was getting farther away by the minute. My head pounded from all the crying and I must have been quite a vision with puffy eyes and lopsided hair. I had no idea where we were and it did not matter, the journey would cover half a continent. I ached with loss, spending most of the next three days in the compartment.

The rest of the family enjoyed the trip, especially the food. On the train, we could order anything we wanted—luxuries like cream on our cereal, fruit, orange juice, and dessert. When I picked at my food, Dad scolded me for being wasteful. His patience was wearing thin. When the train reached the Wainwright station, we disembarked onto little more than an outpost, a windswept town in oil country. It was one of the largest Army camps in Canada, but the town itself had only two thousand people or so. Main Street was dirt, like in some Western movie where people get muddy every time it rains. I realized that this was even *worse* than I thought it would be. Our new home felt lonesome and bare. Fresh tears streamed down my cheeks.

Upon arrival, though, moping time had to end. My parents were seasoned movers and Dad ran our family like a Sergeant Major. They had a system for setup and we each took our orders, first with the beds, including a set of Army green surplus bunkbeds that Dad picked up for Barb and me. We later painted them pink. Then we unpacked suitcases and boxes. At the end of the day, I should have been too tired for anything, but I wrote Jim a letter before nodding into a deep sleep.

The next day, I placed my love note in the mail and waited to see what time the carrier would come. There would be nothing for me yet, of course, but I wanted to know what time I should check each day. From that point on, my life revolved around racing home and wearing a path back and forth if the postman was delayed.

It took more than two agonizing weeks to get his first letter, addressed to a private nickname he had for me, "34," referring to my bust size.

July 22, 1951
Dearest Norma "34"
I still miss you more every day. I intend to come out at the end of the summer but I will be a little cramped for time. If only you weren't so far away.

You must write and tell me exactly what Wainwright is like. The old drive-in here is just the same but it seems different without a cutie pie I know about four foot eleven, blue eyes and hubba hubba.

I hope that you won't forget to write as much as you can. You write a very neat and well paragraphed letter. Would you like a job as a private secretary that is very private when I am finished with school?

I haven't found another girlfriend and I have no intention of doing so. Another girl could never substitute for you. I wouldn't have time to look around anyway as I am trying to save money to come out and see you at the end of the summer.

Norma, oh! I would give my right arm just to be able to hold you in my arms and just kiss you one more time. (Once more, I mean a million times.)

I have said this so many times that you must be tired of reading it, but I love you. To me, Dutch, this is the real thing. In fact, as far as I am concerned you are the one and only for me. A day doesn't go by that some person asks after you and how you are getting along. If only you had been able to stay in Britannia for the rest of the summer we could have had a wonderful time together. But don't forget what I said in Freddie's car the night you were leaving. Well, anyhow, I meant every word of it.

All my love,
Jim
XXXXX times sixty thousand and one.
P.S. Give my regards to your mother and father and the kids.

We sent each other new letters each week and that fall I enrolled in high school. I found that commercial subjects were not offered, so I took those classes at the local Catholic school. That was nice because they had a Friday night dance like I had become accustomed to in Britannia.

I felt nervous about my first dance because I did not know many people yet. After turning sixteen, I graduated to real nylon stockings and Mum knitted me a cream sweater with a popcorn stitch. It had a wide neck and rested just off the shoulders, which I paired with a slim black taffeta skirt. I felt good that night and took a deep breath before stepping inside. The scene came as a bit of a culture shock. Rather than playing waltzes or the foxtrot, three guys stood on a stage wearing long john underwear and playing guitars. I might have turned my nose up at it, but when in Rome, I would learn to square dance.

The new girl always gets some attention and people were so nice, eager to teach me the dances. I found myself swinging in and out of tall people, breathless. After many somber weeks, it felt wonderful to let loose. I could have danced all night, but the band tapered off and I fanned myself. I must have been five pounds lighter, and my new nylon stockings were shredded. Dad would have my hide. It was worth it.

On the way home, I cataloged the evening, thinking of the details I would tell Jim in my next letter. Letters were my new method for reading the world, storing tidbits in my mind to share with him. I saved up observations that I felt only he would understand. If I couldn't tell Jim, it seemed as if it didn't happen. I liked to lay in the grass and look up at the North Star and think of Jim doing the same.

Once in a while I got asked on a date, but I let everyone know I had a boyfriend in Ottawa. Jim and I had agreed not to miss social activities so we both went out, but I never took real interest in anyone else.

Before the next school year, Jim left Britannia, which always felt like our hometown, even though we would never live there again. He moved to Toronto to attend Oakwood Collegiate and live with his Aunt Jean and Uncle Jack Robertson and his three cousins. He packed his best worldly possessions into a big trunk including an antique movie projector, as many books as he could fit, and his clothes.

After Jim got settled, he sent this letter:

September 4, 1951

I have been exceptionally busy, so I won't be able to see you soon but there is no doubt about seeing you next summer as I am pretty sure about a job in Jasper.

Remember the surprise party they threw for you? Well, they held another one for me, and what a surprise! I hadn't had the slightest inclination of what was going on. They gave me a beautiful lighter which was very nice.

My aunt and uncle are really swell to me. I have two sisters and a brother now (cousins). My aunt has some old records that bring back so many nice memories, "My heart beats for you."

You must believe me, Dutch. I still love you very much. I certainly can't tell you how much I have missed you this summer.

I have enclosed a picture taken of me recently (ugh). If you have one of yourself please send me one.

All my love,
Jim
XXXX times every rock on Old Smoky (remember our song), and believe me it's a big mountain

His Aunt Jean and Uncle Jack's home was on Connolly Street of Toronto's West End, a three bedroom, one-bath house. They were the kind of family who welcomed stray friends and animals. The house sat on a postage stamp lot so the family dubbed it Connolly Acres in jest, but it was a lively place with music, dancing, and cards every Friday night. They played ballads on Aunt Jean's record player—anything by the Ink Spots, or the Platters for the kids. Jim shared a room with his youngest cousin Jimmy while the two girls shared the other room, and his aunt and uncle were in the third.

Jim enjoyed having "siblings" and he regaled them with stories, tried to dispense advice, and led outings to Sunnyside Park with its rides and candy floss. His otherwise fun-loving aunt refused to get on the rides, so Jim chaperoned.

That winter, Wainwright made Ottawa seem mild. On the open plains, we had months of bitter cold. We found recreation in ice skating, sleigh rides, and dances. As it warmed up, on Saturday nights Dad would squish us into our tiny British Prefect and we parked on snow-packed Main Street to watch the action. It was like a live action Western watching soldiers pick up girls and bar fights with broken windows. Afterward we would get ice cream.

Dad shuttled us kids to so many sports activities he would mutter, "All I am is a (bleepity) taxi driver."

Jim and I both applied for jobs in Jasper National Park the next summer and he was hired on, but I was stuck in that hellhole because you had to be 18 to work at the park. The only silver lining was that on his way through, Jim's train pulled into the Wainwright station and he could stay with our family. So at 2:15 a.m., my dad and I greeted him on the platform. After a week, we had to part again, and he was off for a summer of work and fun with many of the old gang who got jobs there.

Jim drove a laundry truck at the Jasper Park Lodge, a grand log hotel where the King and Queen of England had stayed. The guys each took a turn lying in the bed where royalty had slept. While Jim was there, the hotel went up in a ravaging fire, its curling fingers of flame licking the sky while the evacuated staff watched billowing smoke for miles. The sound roared above all forest noises, scattering wildlife. Such a disaster brands awe into a person, a new understanding of Mother Nature's fury and the charred devastation she can leave. The sound is unforgettable and the smell of charred rubble triggers vivid memories decades later.

For my 17th birthday, I hatched an idea. Since my mum's relatives were in Vancouver, I could board the train in Edmonton, Dad's new posting. The train stopped in Jasper for Jim to board and we could continue to Vancouver together to stay with relatives for a week together. I took the idea to Mum and she thought for a minute while I bit my lip. She nodded, knowing how heartsick I had been. I think she also felt it was time to entrust me with more responsibility. I postponed asking Dad, but took the risk by buying tickets. What if he said no? I could not bear it. I had some time to find words for my dad, knowing he would dislike the idea. I played various conversations in my head.

The next morning, I went to breakfast with Dad and finally told him.

"Dad, I want to visit Aunt Betty with Jim. She is expecting us." His face turned stern and he paused for a long time before speaking. I held my breath.

"Your mum know about this?" he asked. I nodded while he studied me, "Thought so." He considered further and my heart pounded while thinking, *Please, Dad. I'll die if you say no.* He then said, "Are you asking or telling? Because it seems like you're telling."

I swallowed hard and said, "I'm asking." Another long pause while his lips moved as if to speak and then said nothing.

After a long time, his words were careful and firm. "I do not approve of this. You are only 17 and you still abide by my rules."

My heart sank and I blinked back tears, but he stopped me from getting up.

"I am not finished," he said. "I do not approve, but 17 is old enough to take responsibility. You are a good girl, and I hope you will do as we have taught on your trip."

I wanted to leap up and fling my arms around him in wild gratitude. Instead I said, "I will behave myself." I hugged him and said, "I love you, Dad."

He took me to the train station and we waited together. Now I just enjoyed being with him, the two of us. I was a daddy's girl. I wondered how much more time we would have together before I would start a household of my own. Girlhood memories passed through me, as if embarking on that train marked a new era. It was my first trip with Jim. I felt giddy, yet surprised by this other feeling, as if a chapter were closing. As I waited, I realized that I felt more grown up than when we moved from Britannia, and very different still from the night of that terrible accident. I think my dad sensed it, too. I hardly contained my exuberance for the train to arrive, yet a part of me did not want to leave my dad behind either. We finally heard the train coming and after lumbering to a stop, Dad helped me up the steps. Just moments later, the train—and my life—gained momentum toward Jim Kier.

I took my seat, and the last stretch of waiting had begun. The closer I got, the more I felt like a shook-up Coke, ready to froth over once we stopped. I rather enjoyed the anticipation. I was on my own, watching the scenery, and chatting with other passengers. I sat with an older gentleman, a grandpa sort of man, and I told him how I couldn't wait to see my boyfriend in Jasper. The man was very nice and said, "If he does not board at the station, you are welcome to finish your journey in my company."

I smiled and said, "Thank you, that is very kind," but I knew Jim would be there.

The train began an ascent into the Canadian Rockies, cutting a path through pines and lakes—such a breathtaking contrast to Alberta. As the Jasper station came into view, I spotted a figure standing calm in his bomber jacket. I waited like a rabbit, ready to spring out. I contained myself, though, because Jim was never one for public displays.

Finally, we were together in the best moment I could imagine. Jim looked wonderful and I felt at rest for the first time since leaving Britannia. Time could suspend its funny tricks and just let us enjoy the scenery. When Jim stepped onto that train, I felt like I could finally throw open the windows after a dreary Wainwright winter, leaving my soul awash with fresh sunshine and breeze. Where before I needed to numb the sting of his absence, having him sit beside me heightened every color, sound, and smell.

I thought we might take hours catching up, but our letters had kept each other apprised of the broad brush strokes of life. Jim brought a newspaper article about Freddie Goodfellow, who had joined the military and trained as a pilot. The headline read: "Halifax—Plane nose dives into Maritime bush; Ottawa pilot 22 injured." Freddie was that pilot and had been pulled from the freezing wreck. He was now undergoing a series of surgeries on what had been flawless features. Jim said, "That cat is lucky to be on this side of the grass. This is one of nine lives."

We settled into comfortable silences as the train chugged along, sitting close enough to take in the smell of him, clean soap, leather, and shaving cream. We had been famished for each other. When we entered each long tunnel, the whole train went dark, presenting an opportunity to get close.

We stayed in Vancouver with my Uncle Alec, my Dad's older brother, and Aunt Betty. Then we caught the ferry to beautiful Victoria where I was born and stayed with my Aunt Betty—Auntie Betts—Mum's identical twin.

During that week, we made plans. Upon return, we would work as much as possible and put aside every penny for our life together. We set a savings goal of $1,000 before getting married, but even with combined paychecks, it would take a while. We had the motivation.

Late one evening, we walked along the waterfront in Victoria, awash in the Pacific sea breeze and the pines of Vancouver Island forest. Marine-layer clouds swirled like candy floss stretched wide until it comes apart. Behind was a black sky and twinkling stars. It brought me back to childhood on Shawnigan Lake and Jim listened to me describe the "Shangri La" period.

Jim seemed enthralled in new details of my childhood, so different than his own. We looked across the water together and Jim opened up in an uncharacteristic way.

"I never had a dad, and my mum was unable to make everything okay. She sometimes left me alone. When I think of her problems, I wonder. Maybe we shouldn't have kids. I don't want to pass that on."

I did not know how to respond, so he continued. "Life is frail, but I will always be strong for you."

He trailed off and when I touched his arm, he came back and said, "When I was little, Grandmother swooped in and took me, thank God. I owe everything to her. She was so loving. She had been the manager of a hotel in Scotland before she married. Quite a lady."

He thought for a minute and then continued. "I was named after her husband, my grandfather James E. Kier. I have an ale bottle with my name on it because that was his business."

I remembered that I did not know what the E in his middle name stood for. I had asked before and he had said, "I hate it," and that was the end of the conversation.

I had to find out now, so I prodded, "You get the 'E' from your grandfather, too?"

Jim flicked his hair back. I wheedled, "What does it stand for?"

He laughed, stuck out his chest and said in a Scottish accent, "Yer off yer hed if ya think I'm tellin' ya, lassie."

I laughed at his spot-on brogue, but wasn't about to let him off the hook. "If I'm to be Mrs. James E. Kier, I should know. Out with it!"

He laughed again and spilled the beans. "The E's fer Espie, lassie."

I smiled and I said, "I like the sound of it. What does it mean?"

He shook his head, "No idea, girl."

Now he was back to his own voice, "I'm proud of my Scottish heritage. My Great Grandfather was a businessman and Mayor in Falkirk Scotland. But Espie is an odd name and I hate it. So don't you dare tell anybody." I sealed my lips with a finger.

I wanted him to keep talking so I asked, "Did your grandfather immigrate to Canada?"

Jim shook his head. "He died when my mum and her sister were still little. It must have been a hard time. The girls ended up in an orphanage for a while, but Grandmother pulled through and sometime before 1920 the three sailed for Ontario." He was burrowing into a place that he never opened. "I thought Grandmother would always be here, but when I was 14, her heart got bad and she went to live with her daughter. That's my Aunt Jean."

He searched for words, then stopped. "What is it?" I asked.

He finally confessed a profound regret. "My cousins were there; Aunt Jean was there. Even my mum was around. But when Grandmother died, I was in Britannia. I never got to say goodbye. Maybe Freddie Goodfellow was right. Maybe nothing lasts." Tears were streaming down his cheeks. It would be the *only* time I would see James E. Kier cry. The only time ever.

The next day, Jim was back to his jovial self, but I felt closer to him than ever. He had let me in.

The trip was a dream and it ended way too quickly. In early fall, Jim went back to Toronto for a short time. The next time we saw each other was Christmas when Jim and three of his friends delivered a new car to Vancouver. They had dubbed it the Marilyn Monroe and they all stayed in our home for a singular rowdy night. They brought with them an air of young men heading west to seek their fortunes. After that, Jim was northbound for a job at Gunner Gold Mine in Saskatchewan way up near the border of Northwest Territory. It's the sort of place where harsh conditions meant good pay for a young man who knew how to work.

After high school in 1952, I got a job as a teletype operator for the Army in the Signal Corps in Wainwright. Then Dad got transferred to Edmonton and the family left with him, but I stayed put for a bit. The first moment I was eligible, I applied for a transfer and was soon able to follow them to the bustling city of Edmonton, the sixth-largest metro area in Canada. Shortly after that, our whole family was living together again in Army housing called Griesbach Barracks. I was so happy to be back in civilization.

I loved going dancing with my girlfriends, especially with a girl named Jenny. There were several new dinner-dance nightclubs with the wonderful big band music of the time. We particularly liked a fancy one called the Trocadero, the place to be in Edmonton. With Jim still away, I often brought my brother Jon who was a fine dancer and made an excellent partner for me. We always had such a good time together.

I enjoyed office work and was amused by the bawdy Army environment. I kept most of the jokes to myself, but occasionally as Mum, Barb and I washed dishes, I might repeat one of the milder jokes. Barb and I would burst into laughter and Mum just kept washing as if she had not heard. An English lady *does not laugh* at coarse humor.

I sent Jim things to make his life up north more comfortable and knitted a heavy woolen sweater with a bear and tree pattern. I guess there is a wives' tale that it is bad luck to knit something for a beau, but he wore it a lot and still had it in his closet sixty years later.

I continued to write and I sent him this letter:

Dear Jim,

Here it is Sunday again, and I'm back in bed. I wish you were here with me. Jim, I love you so much. I've said it a thousand times before and I'll say a thousand times more. I only wish I could say it in person instead of writing it on a piece of paper. But just you wait. Someday I'll say it so much you will get tired of hearing it. I hope you don't though.

How are you holding up against the cold weather? Has it gone any colder than 50 below yet? The weather here isn't much warmer. Yesterday when I went to work it was 32 below. I thought for sure I'd freeze before I got to work. I had to catch the bus and transfer three times before I made it to work okay.

Jim, it's torture being kept apart. I love you so much and want to be with you always. I can't think of a better way to spend my lifetime than with you. I am always dreaming & wishing things like that. Someday I hope they all come true.

Who knows what the future will bring? I have my fingers crossed. Lots of love, Jim. See you in my dreams.

All my love,
XXXXXXX Norma
P.S. Do you really feed the wolves?

Later that year, Jim finally moved down to Edmonton for a job building homes with an American construction company. Mum and Dad let him sleep on our sofa until he found a place of his own, renting a room in a boarding house with other young men. One was named Bob Ross and he became a good friend in no time. I introduced Bob to my friend Jenny and they started dating.

The four of us often went on double dates and Bob entertained us with antics like when we sat on the second-floor balcony of the Trocadero, he liked to flick ice onto the dancers below. He'd then duck before being seen. One time he stepped out into traffic and acted like a police officer directing cars around him with big funny gestures. Jenny was a quiet, good sport. Jim would laugh with his whole body, but wasn't generally a major rule breaker himself.

We always closed the dance floor. Jim never minded me dancing with anybody else, although he would cut in if he thought it necessary. The song "Save the Last Dance for Me," comes to mind.

On July 22, 1955, after Jim and I had just turned 24 and 20, we went out with Jenny and Bob to a new dance-and-dine club called the Isle of Capri. Jenny and I wore cocktail dresses and the men had on jackets with ties. We ordered items like Salisbury steak and Hawaiian pork over rice. Before our entrées were served, Jenny and I went to the powder room.

After returning, Jim asked me for a comb, so I fished one out of my purse. When I handed it over, he looked at me kind of funny. A few minutes later, he asked for a stick of gum and seemed surprised when I handed him one. Then he asked for my handkerchief. That time when I got in my purse, I saw something that had not been there before, a black velvet case with a metal hinge. My heart began to pound.

"What's this?" I asked, and he was already getting on one knee. I flushed with joy.

He asked me to marry him and I said an emphatic "Yes!" Then he placed the ring on my finger.

We were finished with all this waiting business.

The lights were soft while music drifted across the room, although that dim lighting was to blame for what happened next. I gazed at my beautiful new ring and with misty eyes I said, "I only wish I could see it!"

Jim looked wounded, wondering if he should take it back. I simply meant I wanted to admire it in proper light. I was over the moon, and when I realized my faux pas, I said a hundred apologies. Dumb. Dumb. Dumb. If it hurt his feelings, though, he did not let it ruin our happiness. We danced to every song, working on our Jitterbug until janitors came out with big brooms. Before we left, the staff gave us a lovely salt and pepper shaker set in congratulations.

After four long years since the train left Britannia, I could tell my family I was engaged. Our wedding would be in a year.

Around that time, my parents thought it might help me conquer shyness to enroll in a modeling course at the Peggy Adams Modeling school. I learned to walk with correct posture and other elements of grace, including how to pose for a photograph. It did give me a great deal more confidence and the staff encouraged me to sign up for the Miss Eskimo Pageant, associated with the Edmonton Eskimos pro football team (like the NFL in the States). I hesitated when I realized it meant being in front of all those people, but let myself be persuaded out of my shell. If I could settle my nerves, it might even be fun.

On the night of the big pageant, Jim gave me flowers and I received telegrams from friends and relatives all over Canada. I was so nervous, but can you believe that I was selected as a finalist? This would give me many opportunities over the coming months and I kept pinching myself.

When the picture came out in the paper, I received calls from guys who wanted to know if that was a ring on my finger. Jim cheered me every step, like the time we rode in convertibles for a parade. Jim ran along the sidewalk snapping as many pictures as he could before the car inched out of view.

Mum let me borrow her fur coat to go to a fancy tea with the football players' wives. For another event, an Army Colonel picked me up in an official car to drive to the University. I was dressed in a female Army uniform and in a little sketch I had to walk out, salute the Colonel, and give him a message. I nearly poked my eye out saluting and my knees buckled in front of a large audience. On another day, the girls—who were all so very nice—went on a radio program with the star quarterback.

What a thrilling year building up to our wedding. Jim and I saved as much as we could, and Mum did too, although we were nowhere near our $1,000 goal. We set a date for Labor Day weekend, September 1, 1956, and Mum helped me pick out a lovely white lace dress with ruffles. What a sacrifice for my parents to come up with $79.95, a generous luxury on my behalf. We had made it five years since Jim first proposed on my sixteenth birthday the night our train left for Wainwright.

A few days before, Mum made the bride's cake using a traditional fruitcake recipe which was dense enough to hold the weight of tiers. She went to the cupboard for rum and heaved a great sigh. It was gone and she knew where. Having been caught, Dad dashed to get another bottle while my siblings and I chopped up the fruit. Mum then took the baked cake to a decorator.

The ceremony was held in our church, the United Church of Canada in Griesbach Barracks. On the way to the chapel, Bob drove Jim and they got stopped by a freight train. Does anything feel slower than a decelerating train when you must be somewhere? Boxcars nudged along and Bob grinned, saying, "Here it is. Your last chance to make a break."

They got there on time.

My siblings were all part of the wedding party with everyone wearing their Sunday best. Bob was Jim's best man and my girlfriend Noreen was my Maid of Honor. As we said, "I do," my nerves made my voice so quiet that I almost couldn't be heard. After, we walked toward Dad's car to borrow it for the honeymoon but I stopped in front a big mud puddle. Jim knew what to do, swooping me into his arms and carrying me across. A camera caught the moment.

We could finally begin our life together, marked by a brief honeymoon in Jasper and Banff. Dad let us borrow his car since we didn't have one. Also, we could not afford any grand Lodge where the Queen might make an appearance, but were happy in a cute little cabin in Jasper instead. Then it was off to Banff and back home to play house in a small apartment. We decorated with a few furnishings we bought with our savings, including a chrome table with red chairs and some furniture borrowed from Mum and Dad in the living room.

Jenny and Bob were married two months after we were, in the same church and by the same Army chaplain. This time we stood up for them.

Jim was still working for that American construction company while I kept on with my teletype job for the Army. A few months later, the construction company made Jim a new offer. They had acquired a piece of property about ten years earlier on the outskirts of Ogden, Utah, in the United States, and had been sitting on it, waiting for the city to grow. The time had come to build homes and they needed a Superintendent for the subdivision project and offered me work as a secretary.

We had the sort of basic knowledge of Utah that every Canadian student gets in school, learning all fifty states, their capital cities and biggest industries. We had grown up watching American television shows and all the Canadian kids at that time wanted to visit the states. Aside from that, Jim had heard from the company that Ogden was a nice enough place at the base of the Rocky Mountains. The details really did not matter much, though. We were game for a big adventure. I was 21 and Jim was 25. We made some temporary storage arrangements for many items including my wedding dress. We knew our apartment would not be very large and it was best to leave things we would not need until our return.

1957 – 1961

OGDEN

———◼———

We piled into a freezing car with Jim's new boss and were greeted by spring in Utah a few days later. It was March of 1957 and we had $100 in our pockets after making our apartment deposit. When we got out of the vehicle in our new town, we found the community absolutely beautiful, much more so than we expected. Crocuses were already out and the smell of an early thaw was in the air. This felt like heaven after Edmonton, which is winter nine months out of the year.

Jim's boss had arranged for our first place and we moved into lucky number 7 of the Revelle apartments which sat on the northwest corner of 25th Street and Monroe Boulevard. It was a tidy one-bedroom that had an unobstructed view looking northeast to the mountains, which we loved. The interior was small and modern with speckled carpet in muted tones and a flecked treatment called Zolatone on the walls. The little kitchen had linoleum floors, white cabinets, and white curtains. Our Formica table with chrome legs and red vinyl chairs was delivered from Canada along with our bedroom set and a few living room items.

Jim went to work as the foreman on the subdivision at the top of 3rd Street in Ogden and I joined him each day doing secretarial work from a trailer office that moved from project to project. Obviously there is no United Church of Canada in Utah, so we inquired around and learned that Trinity Presbyterian Church would be the closest to what we were used to, so we began attending there. It was near the subdivision we were building.

We liked the pace of Ogden, a much smaller city than Edmonton, but it still bustled. Washington Boulevard was a vibrant main street with plenty of nice shopping like Samuel's department store and other little boutiques, not that I was buying clothes at that time. Lower 25th Street was seedy with smoky bars and prostitutes coming out at night. It was not somewhere a woman would walk alone after dark. All this made for entertaining people watching, although with a more urban flavor than Wainwright had been.

Jim and I never splurged on going out to eat—people rarely did in those years—but by the time temperatures started warming, we would take our Friday paycheck, get a hamburger, fries, and milkshake and head up Ogden Canyon where we'd sit on rocks and eat. Since our apartment was not air conditioned, the canyon became a respite and our primary form of entertainment most evenings during the summer. Summer heat in Utah was something else.

As similar as the United States and Canada are, we found ourselves adjusting to subtle differences, including parts of the language you don't expect: "Mom" instead of "Mum," which I never adopted, and how I ended sentences in "eh?" I never broke that habit entirely, although it morphed into "hey," which didn't sound so funny to friends in Ogden. One of the first times I went to the grocery store, the clerk asked if I wanted a "sack" for the groceries and I imagined a burlap sack flung over my shoulder. I said, "No thank you. A paper bag will do."

One evening, we invited another couple for dinner and she asked where we were from. Jim said, "Ontario."

The wife asked, "Oh, is Ontario a big city?"

I explained, "Ontario is the province, like a state. We lived in the city of Ottawa."

She was trying to act interested, "So how big is Ottawa?"

Jim said, "It's the capital of Canada, so the Parliament buildings are there. It's bigger than Salt Lake City." They seemed surprised that Canada had any cities as big as Salt Lake, but even Edmonton was three times the size of Ogden.

Now the husband chimed in. "Parliament and the Queen?"

Jim played along. "Oh yes, the Queen sits on her throne in the Parliament building and everyone drives horse-drawn buggies. Except in the winter when it's all sleighs. It was exciting to move here because we finally got to see television." Jim was cracking up. That night we had a glass of wine, sang a rousing O Canada together, and felt a bit homesick.

At first, we allotted ourselves one brief monthly telephone call to my parents, which triggered a longing for them and for Canada and I would bawl. After a few times of that, Jim said "There's not much point calling home if you're just going to cry." He was right and international calls were very, very expensive, so after a while I mostly wrote letters.

Jim and I had planned to go to Las Vegas over July 4th, which would double as a birthday present to me. Then we realized Mum and Dad were moving to Vancouver after his Army retirement, so we coaxed them into coming down. They drove Dad's car and brought my sister Barb, who was 16 at the time. They camped in sleeping bags and foam rubber mats in the living room and we became more aware that there was no door to our bedroom, an odd setup that hadn't bothered us before.

Then we all piled into Dad's car for Vegas. It was our first desert summer and we really had no reference point as to what Las Vegas in July meant. Dad's car lacked air conditioning, which was more common in Canada then. As we drove, the car got hotter than hell, so Barb and I put our feet outside the back windows.

At about St. George, a police siren whirred and he told us to put our legs back in the car.

"You'll distract other motorists."

We wanted to explain that a couple of Canadian girls might die back there.

At Mesquite, Dad's car overheated and we had to add more water to the radiator as Dad mumbled, "What are you doing in this God forsaken place?"

I laughed him off, saying, "Think of how much worse it could be."

Barb was skeptical, "*Do* tell."

I responded, "Winter in Wainwright, running to the outhouse." Compared to the present oven, though, anything cool sounded more like a fantasy.

We made it to Las Vegas and even in the heat, we were dazzled by the strip. It was worth seeing, just maybe not in July. While there, we got ready for a show, and I felt brave enough to wear a low-cut dress thinking

I should be able to get away with it in Las Vegas. When Jim looked at me, his face went stern. It would take some time in our marriage before he was ready for his wife to wear anything in public that hinted at sexy.

Just like that, the trip was over. Mum, Dad, and Barb left and I cried buckets.

After reaching a milestone on the subdivision project, Jim's boss and his wife took us to dinner at Maddox in Brigham City. I panned the menu for something inexpensive, but he said, "And a steak for the little lady."

I had never eaten a steak in my entire life and I practically closed my eyes to enjoy every morsel. I made mental notes of the entire meal so I could write my parents about it and I had the waiter wrap leftovers for me. After dinner, I looked around the restaurant for a band or something so we could dance off the meal as we were accustomed to in such a nice place. I was disappointed to not find one, so we just sat tight while Jim's boss ordered himself round after round of drinks, even though we stopped early.

He loosened up and said, "I don't know how the two of you work for the same company. No offense, honey," he said turning to his wife, "But if we worked together, we'd kill each other. Business and family don't mix."

The tab that night could have paid our rent.

We made it through our first winter in Ogden, which basically felt like springtime in Edmonton. Whenever anyone said, "It's so cold out," I would say, "You don't know what cold really is."

About the time of Utah's earliest thaw, a feeling of nausea came over me, so I went to see the doctor. He confirmed that I was three months pregnant. When I told Jim, we danced around the apartment. By that time, Jim had decided to set aside his fears about having children, and we were ready.

"I promise you I will be strong enough to face anything life throws at us," he said.

I phoned Mum and Dad who were elated to learn of their first grandchild on the way. A few days later, they sent a telegram, formally marking the occasion. It said, "Congratulations! We were beginning to wonder." That was Dad for you.

I had a friend at the time who was also pregnant, and when summer days got warm in the apartment, we went down the stairs of the Revelle Apartments and visited the drug store on the street level of our building. We greeted Mr. Revelle and his son who ran it, and then treated ourselves to a chocolate milkshake on the steps. Before we started to show, we often walked over to Lester Park to work on our tans, but by mid-summer we were resting more modestly in the shade.

Some of my friends might only gain fifteen pounds during pregnancy, but I put on 35, and I complained about this to the doctor. He reassured me that when you start out only weighing 98 pounds, your body needs to add a little more.

"You'll take it right off." My ankles never swelled, though, and when you looked at me from behind, it was hard to tell I was pregnant. Small as I was, my body seemed made to have babies.

I made a shopping trip to Sears downtown to buy the layette set. With my mum being a twin, I had this feeling I had better put twin insurance on it so if I had twins they would double everything at no extra cost. Those were good gambling odds for Sears because twins were quite uncommon at that time.

On the way home, I got a whiff of baked goods from the Hostess factory, normally a pleasant experience in that part of town, but this time I took shallow breaths all the way home to keep from throwing up. *Hurry, hurry, hurry.* I fumbled with the key, dumped my bags in the doorway, and went straight to the toilet. I stood there and finally opened my mouth. Out came a burp. That was the end of it and the closest I ever came to morning sickness in my life.

Jim's superintendent job kept him busy building the subdivision and I continued to work in the office. We picked out a lot for ourselves and began building our first home. What a blessing to be in a career that would make this possible at our age. We were also making many new friends. One instant connection was a man about Jim's age named Bill Wood who worked for Prudential Federal Savings. He was writing the construction loans for the subdivision homes and came out to inspect the properties as they were finished. He and Jim hit it off, so they scheduled inspections for quitting time so they could meet for a drink, a laugh, and to cut loose a little. Bill was smart, quick to talk politics, and an instigator of fun. These qualities were something of a theme in Jim's close buddies: Freddie Goodfellow, Bob Ross, and now Bill Wood.

In late summer, Jim's eldest cousin Joan, who was about six years younger than Jim, wrote asking if she could visit after nursing school and on her way to a job at Cedars of Lebanon in Los Angeles. I was so excited to meet her. This was to be the first member of Jim's family I had ever met, and she planned to stay for nearly a month. Jim said, "You'll like her."

I welcomed her with a big hug and I thought she was both pretty and warm. Jim was right; I did take to her right away. I could see why the family joked that Jim and Joan made a handsome couple, although she had lovely blonde hair in contrast to his black mop. When I pulled out the sleeping bag, she joked about how they ran a veritable bed and breakfast at Connolly Acres, all it took was a sleeping bag or two.

Cousin Joan and I went for walks and I asked questions about their family. In that month, I learned more about Jim's past than he had ever told me.

"Jim is named after our grandfather, who died in Scotland. After he died, our grandmother had some family income and a brother in Canada, so she and her two girls set off. That was in the 20s, and our mums were still little. There must have been some ups and downs because Grandmother and the girls went back to Scotland once, but finally settled in Britannia."

I got brave and asked about Jim's mother. Jim always referred to her as "Dorothy" and never "Mum." Joan obliged and told me more.

"Dorothy was a real beauty but by the time she finished high school, she was already showing signs of trouble. I don't think she was quite right even then."

Then I asked Joan about her own Mum, Jim's Aunt Jean. Joan said, "My mum was the younger sister and she married in her mid-teens. I think she wanted someone to take care of her, and my dad does. When my parents moved to Toronto as a young couple, I think it was hard on Grandmother to have her only stable daughter move away. Grandmother and my mum were close their whole lives."

I asked Joan, "How often did you all visit Britannia?"

Joan answered, "We came a lot. It's about four hours by train. The best part was seeing cousin Jimmy. We idolized him and his friends."

We enjoyed our time while Joan was in Ogden, but late summer heat in Utah came as a great shock to her. The summer heat was hard on me, too, as my pregnancy progressed. By August, the apartment was sweltering, so the three of us packed our station wagon, which we had purchased on our first anniversary, and headed out to Yellowstone.

The park teemed with families undertaking the great summer of the late 1950s, hitting national parks and Disneyland. Cooler temperatures felt like home, and we called out any Canadian license plate we spotted. Jim found us a campsite close to the outhouse restrooms so I could make it in the middle of the night now that I was so pregnant. The smell left something to be desired, though. We made camp and Jim fashioned beds with sleeping bags and foam mattresses in the back of the station wagon to make me comfortable. I didn't mind at all. We were happy to be together, and not in the hot apartment.

We roasted hot dogs and after Jim had a beer or two, the stories began.

Joan said, "Remember when you and all those friends came to the Grey Cup game in Toronto?"

Jim said, "The time Ottawa was in it."

Joan told me, "Jimmy must have brought a dozen guys and gals from that gang you all palled around with in Ottawa. Did anybody even have a ticket?"

Jim shook his head and Joan went on. "What a party. I remember going to the bathroom the next morning and there was some poor sap sleeping in the bathtub. In the bathtub!"

Jim grinned, "I still owe your parents for that."

Joan seemed nostalgic, "We had some great parties at Connolly Acres."

Jim added, "Your mum and dad are terrific. I want a home that feels like that for our children."

His mood was shifting and as the fire quieted, he asked, "What do you remember about our Grandmother?"

Joan answered, "When she moved in with us, I was still young and her health was not good. She took meals in her own room, she was kind, and I remember her telling us fairy tales. She taught me how to make paper flowers from her bed. I wish I knew her as well as you did."

Jim nodded and Joan continued. "Oh, I remember this. She was following this big murder case in the papers. One night there was a power outage, and we had candles everywhere. She had me get the paper to read about it by candle. She died that night."

A weight had settled over Jim and I could sense him retreating into himself. Joan added, "That was a sad time. Grandmother was gone and my mum got hospitalized for a while after that. That's when Dorothy came to help."

Jim said, "Grandmother looked after me, but before she died, she made your mum promise to look after Dorothy. It must have been doubly hard for your mum, losing Grandmother and having the added burden of Dorothy. It must have pushed her over the edge."

Joan nodded, "Yes, but Dorothy pulled it together enough when we needed her. When I think of the time after Grandmother's death, I can always see those candles in my mind."

She was quiet for a few minutes before adding, "When our mums were in the orphanage, they set out candles whenever someone died. Candles haunted them after that."

I got brave and asked, "How is she?"

Joan said, "Oh my mum is great now. You'd never know she had a hard time then."

I shook my head and Joan said, "Oh, you mean Dorothy. About the same. There, but not there. She helps my mum with errands, but she doesn't live in the same world as the rest of us."

The flames had died, the embers were cooling, and Jim's gaze focused somewhere out in the forest. He stood up, tossed empties into the trash, and we retired to sleeping bags.

We returned home, wished Joan well in her new endeavors, and got ready to welcome a baby. Through late September, I was having labor pains, and when I was certain they were real, we rushed to the hospital late in the evening of October 6. We got to the hospital around 11:30, and at check-in, the nice lady looked at the clock.

She leaned in with a hushed voice saying, "If your labor pains are not that bad, it will save you an entire day's bill to check in after midnight." Jim looked my way with concern, but I held up my hand.

"I'm fine. Maybe it won't even happen tonight." We waited in the lobby until 12:02 and then checked in like we had all the time in the world. My abdomen was tightening hard, then loosening at regular intervals. The hospital staff helped me into a delivery room and directed Jim to the area where fathers waited, paced, and fidgeted with the cellophane on cigars.

With the blessing of a hypodermic shot, I had a clockwork delivery. Stephen James Kier was born at 8:30 the next morning, making his birthday October 7, 1958. He was perfect in every regard, right down to teeny-tiny fingernails and soft eyelashes. What a flood of joy, relief, and a hushed sacred feeling of holding a new life. I was part of a mother-child bond that would exist forevermore. They invited Jim back into the room to meet his son, who weighed 6 pounds, 14 ½ ounces. Jim was very, very proud of the little guy, if a little tentative about what to do. He had never been around babies and didn't want to break him. Also, what a relief it was that twin insurance had not been required.

Jim visited us and enjoyed every delightful moment with his baby, but I could see little droplets of sweat. "Are you okay?" I asked.

He responded, "Fine. It's just the smell and the beeping and people shuffling about. It makes me queasy."

I smiled, "I never would have guessed when you visited me in the hospital in Ottawa."

He looked boyish while holding Steve. "That was young love," he said, then nestled his nose into the crook of our baby's head and neck. Yes, new love was a good way for describing what we felt for Steve, but magnified.

A nurse opened the door and he startled. "May I check vitals?"

I nodded and turned toward Jim, "I think you should go get some rest. I'm in good hands here."

He looked relieved, "You did great," he said and dashed out, a little worse for the wear.

From the moment Steve arrived, he went after life with voracious intensity, knowing what he needed and nearly always getting it by asking, reminding, or even fighting for it. He was a lot like Jim: a born athlete and a natural leader. He would be articulate like Jim, but less reserved, and he was the first of our children to inherit that little bit of hell that comes from my side, the Jessimans. Each one of us in our own way.

We adjusted to the new responsibility and with me being an eldest child, I had plenty of experience with children. Jim was less confident, but still eager. He never had a father's example to follow, but from the first moment, he was involved and protective. As winter approached, something in the apartment began to really bother us. The apartment manager turned the heat completely off at ten o'clock each night and did not start it again until six a.m. This was troubling with a tiny baby, and it made us angry that the manager would treat tenants that way, so cheap we could not even keep our newborn warm. We were relieved that our first home was ready to move in just before Thanksgiving. It was 980 finished square feet and part of the subdivision Jim was building. Our house was at the top of Third Street at 1332 3rd, just behind the LDS church and near Trinity Presbyterian.

We were looking forward to moving in and hosting American Thanksgiving dinner in our new place. Canadian Thanksgiving had already passed in October, which I always liked because it was separated a little more from Christmas.

We moved in at the first possible moment, but at the end of November, the water line had not quite reached our home yet. Jim stretched a hose from the main line a half block away. It was a small inconvenience, but I knew the drill from Mum hauling water inside most of her life. This would be temporary for us, while it had been a permanent chore in Mum's life. We also had the comfort of central heat that we controlled, and I would never have to get up in a freezing house before dawn to start the stove. We were so blessed.

The night before Thanksgiving got very cold and we worried about the hose freezing. We left it dripping, but when we awoke, there was a solid icicle from the spout. It took some finagling, but Jim got water in time for our dinner with guests.

On a day of thanks, we acknowledged what a life we already had: good jobs, a new home, and a baby. After waiting so long to be together, I think we appreciated each other more than many couples. In 1958, it felt like our little family participated in a wave of optimism and new beginnings that washed across North America. We were building a subdivision as part of it. The next months were all about adjusting to a baby and Jim working, with me still on payroll to choose colors and finishes for the homes.

For my birthday the following summer, with Steve just nine months old, I got the same wonderful present as the year before—a visit from family. My sister Barb took a bus down and stayed with us for a week. When she got here, we hugged and danced around, two young women who had once huddled under blankets together for warmth and who looked like exact copies except for a few years between us. She was exuberant to meet her first nephew, too, and Steve took right to his aunt.

Just before my actual birthday, Jim announced, "Barb and I have business in town." He had asked her to accompany him shopping because he wanted help picking out clothes for me. Barb had grown up so much since the days when she pestered Jim and his buddies at the end of the pier.

Out shopping, Barb and Jim had an easy form of banter, genuinely enjoying each other's company. In the store, she picked a cute candy striped two-piece outfit and Jim nodded, "Definitely the one."

There were two similar versions, and she asked, "Which one do you like best?"

"Both," he said.

She tilted her head and he grinned.

"You would look so pretty in it; I want you to have one, too." So she chose one style for me and the other for herself, lighting up at the surprise.

Around that same time, Mum and Dad drove down from Vancouver. It was the first time they had seen their grandson. They adored him and Dad sized Steve up, even doting, "You are a very strong boy. What sports will you play?" We got a babysitter for the very first time ever and the four of us went to dinner. They also watched him a time or two so Jim and I could have a little time alone.

They returned home and I soon got word that the place we had been storing belongings in Canada had a fire. My wedding dress and other keepsakes had been waiting for our return, but they were gone now.

I hoped it wasn't a bad omen, but we received a $100 insurance check and used the money to buy a high chair.

Before we knew it, Steve had turned one and I became pregnant again. We were thrilled, but suddenly nervous about our employment situation as we had begun noticing signs of trouble in our boss. He'd go on a bender and be MIA for a while before turning up and acting like nothing had happened. We could sense people at the bank whispering.

Jim confided in me, "I'm getting concerned for our reputation. It might be time to go back home." That had always been our idea, but we had wanted to accomplish a little more here first. Also, we had it in our minds that we would save money so at the right time, we could branch out on our own. Going back to Canada would certainly be a setback and delay plans to start a business, a disappointment. Our savings were still small, especially with a second baby on the way.

When our boss didn't show up for work again, nobody thought much of it at first. Then one day stretched into a week, then more time passed and he wasn't returning calls. Nobody had heard a word and not even Jim knew how to reach him. Jim did his best to keep everyone busy on the job site while trying to quell the rumor mill, but we were all nervous.

Bill Wood turned up on the building lot and Jim felt sick when he spotted him.

Bill asked, "Have you seen the boss?"

Jim had to shake his head, then turned to Bill, "Have you?"

Bill motioned away from other workers and said, "Let's get lunch." Jim worried if this might be some form of layoff news. The workers eyed them driving away together.

Over sandwiches, Bill filled Jim in. "It appears your boss has been snooting the ol' mash barrel and has in fact, skipped town. Vanished."

Jim tugged at his ear. The boss was responsible for not only Jim's paycheck, but every other worker's too. A lot of people we cared about would be left shivering come winter. Our predicament was the same as theirs: savings would evaporate.

Jim's mind was already working on options to get us back to Canada before the baby came, but Bill interrupted with his company's side of things.

"Prudential is in a pickle. Half that subdivision is unfinished. There are homes waiting to close and families calling every day."

Jim nodded and Bill asked, "What are your plans?"

Jim said, "Go home to Canada, I suppose."

Bill held up his hand in and said, "Please don't. I can tell you that Prudential has a plan, and you're it. You wrap up the subdivision in brown paper and a ribbon."

Jim looked surprised, "Me? I don't have the resources to take this on. And I don't have my license yet."

Bill wasn't fazed. "How long to get your General Contractor's license?"

Jim shook his head, unsure, especially given that studying would take time along with managing the project and having a pregnant wife.

Bill turned up the heat, "Prudential is up shit creek, but I can swing the numbers."

Jim raised an eyebrow, but Bill was confident, "I'll take care of the money. You take care of the subs and families with half-built homes. We all need a guy to trust, and your reputation is ace high."

Jim brushed his upper lip, "I'll talk it over with Norma."

It was a hard decision with mother Canada beckoning, but Jim had a duty and we would see the job through. Then we could go.

The pregnancy progressed and Jim worked like crazy and studied until his eyelids dropped. He got his General Contractor license months before I went into labor.

As the homes were finished one by one, our decision loomed bigger. Now we must start over again in Canada or branch out on our own here. Either decision was unnerving with a young family. It could go either way.

We had the baby on the 4th of July, an all-American boy with Canadian blood. Labor began on my birthday, July 3rd, and Scott John Kier greeted us the next morning. Scott was a healthy 6 pounds, 9 ounces and the cutest little chubby baby. Our love was magnified by two. We were so head-over-heels for these babies it is hard to even put it into words. Absolutely smitten.

Scott was born twenty-one months after Steve, which meant they would be separated by two grades in school, but not by much else. Their names became Steveandscott or "the Kier Boys" almost like one entity, and best buds from the first day. They also did a regular amount of sibling fighting.

I shelved other cares for a little while and doted on the boys. Steve was still just a little tyke, but took to being a big brother. Since he was younger than two when Scott was born, being brothers was all they would ever remember. For their entire childhood they shared a bedroom, fought like mad, explored, instigated, and stood up for each other.

Jim had his license now and was beyond busy finishing the subdivision. With an uncertain future, we socked every penny away but had not saved enough for either plan. I was as committed to our goals as Jim, and glad to do my part. Growing up I never expected lavish clothes or expensive food and that mindset suited us now. I needed very little in the way of wardrobe then, and didn't even own a slip. Everyone has their limits, though, and on a particularly hot day after Scott was born, I opened my closet and slid hangers from left to right. "Too warm," I sighed. "Shabby," and "definitely too stuffy." My clothes were looking faded, and I had a daydream that involved buying a new pair of shorts. The doorbell rang, and I went to find the Winder Dairy milkman there to collect payment. We had a good rapport, and he gave me an extra bottle of milk every time one of my friends signed up for the service.

I asked him to wait for a moment and as I trotted to get my checkbook, I had a bold idea. I returned to the door, pocketbook in hand.

"Would it be possible to make this check for five dollars over the bill?"

"We do it all the time," he said.

I wrote it for the higher amount and he deposited a five-dollar bill in my hand. With a light step, I dragged one toddler and one newborn downtown to purchase for myself—*all for myself*—a new pair of shorts. I pulled them on and felt like a new person, lighter and a bit pampered.

It's not that I had to ask for things, and I knew I could have anything I needed. I was simply judicious with actual needs for myself. We were in partnership together and frugality was a way I could contribute. I did not hesitate to buy what the children needed, but luxuries like new clothes for me seemed frivolous. Every now and again, though, an indulgence felt fantastic. A guilty pleasure.

Later that fall, Jim said, "We're overdue for you to meet Aunt Jean and Uncle Jack."

I lit up. "Toronto! When?"

Jim said, "Maybe Christmas. Scott will be six months and we can spare some savings for ourselves. It's important to see family."

I added, "It can be our Christmas present to each other!" After all this time, I had still only met one of Jim's relatives, his cousin Joan.

Jim said, "You will love them," and he added with a twinkle, "They'll take one look at you and say I married up."

I laughed and squeezed his hand, "You were a good catch, Jimmy Kier." I was thrilled at the idea of Canada and the big city and meeting the rest of my new family.

When the time came to leave, though, our hopes were dashed. Both boys got very sick and there would be no traveling. We had been building it up so much that everyone was disappointed, but we made the best of it and built little tent forts over each of the boy's beds, with a vaporizer going inside. This mini adventure cheered them up; children that age are so easily pleased. It took us longer to brighten, but what can you do? Enjoy Christmas with your children and get back to work; that's what you do.

During the following months, Jim finished up the subdivision and Bill Wood was working on us to stay. He came to dinner a lot, and aside from the friendship—or perhaps because of it—he was a man on a mission. He pushed back his plate one evening saying, "Good groceries, Norma. Thanks for taking pity on me."

I smiled warmly at him, "You're a good egg, Bill."

He chuckled, "Tell my mother that, will you? She always said I was a deportment problem with my citizenship grade."

I nodded, "I will give you a recommendation any time."

Bill narrowed his eyes, like he was all business now, and he turned to Jim. "Will you do me a solid and hang up a shingle? We should do deals together. People say business ruins friendships, but I'd put my life in your hands, man."

Jim twitched his mouth and said, "We are a long way from our savings goal."

47

Bill brushed his hand at Jim, "I'll take care of the moolah." Jim was noncommittal, so Bill prodded, "The good people of Utah like you." Bill Wood truly was the first cheerleader and backer we had.

Around this time, we also became acquainted with a successful businessman by the name of Ben Charlesworth who owned Colorite Inc., a paint company and contractor. Ben was a jovial sort and had a fatherly way with Jim. Ben said to Jim, "You appreciate things and you know how to work. Remember to instill that in your sons. I have a few regrets about how I did things."

We really liked that guy. I remember early on taking a set of plans down for him to bid at his store on 33rd and Wall. Ben took the rolled-up plans, shook the papers like a rain stick, listened for a sound, and grinned. He said, "Eight hundred dollars," as his best and final bid without looking at the details.

When we told Ben we were thinking of going into business, he offered to give us a twenty thousand-dollar loan to buy some property and build a couple of spec homes saying, "This is a bet on you. Make me proud."

We were still a long way from our savings goal to start a business, but I remembered how in Canada, we wanted to save a thousand dollars before getting married. When that loomed as an impossibility, we just took the plunge anyway. Mr. Charlesworth was the second key person to believe in our business and give us a start. This loan and Prudential's commitment to finance construction signaled a vote of confidence to start up. We would stay in Ogden for now.

1961 - 1969

BIRTH OF A BUSINESS

On August 7, 1961, we officially began Kier Construction, a proprietorship of Jim and Norma Kier, headquartered in a 10x10 spare bedroom, our first office.

The first home we built was in North Ogden on Elberta Drive. We also got in touch with a property owner of a bigger parcel nearby where we wanted to build spec homes. We got together with him in person, because we felt it was important to paint a vision for him. The owner was a very nice LDS man, and along the way I became self-conscious about how different we might seem, being from Canada and not as conservative as the prevailing community. When Jim was lit up about something, though, he had a way of making an impression. The man not only agreed to sell us lots, he would do so one at a time, and with only a down payment at the beginning of each home. The balance could be paid when the home sold. He would make a good profit on the land, but it was still very generous and trusting. We were beaming and have been forever grateful for the risk he took on our young family. He was the third key person to bet on our future, allowing us to leverage cash and hold some in reserve for contingencies.

No matter how large or small a construction company is, cash will always be the most precious tangible resource. Protecting it is the first commandment in this business. We began then with a lifelong discipline of squirreling away proceeds from each job to parlay into bigger projects. As young as we were, we had already noticed a tendency for contractors to slip into good times like a warm bath, taking on liabilities that could sink them. Only fools believe the sun will keep shining forever.

During the building phase, Jim often took one or both boys to the job site. One day, he seated Steve at the controls of a tractor and stepped aside to review plans with somebody or other. He turned around and spotted Steve's little sneakers flailing upward, his head out of sight. Our little tyke had crawled into the steering wheel and then got caught, his feet kicking in the air and his cheeks flushed. Jim ran over and rescued the boy, "Sorry, Sorry!"

On our way to the construction site on Elberta Drive, we frequented the Conoco station on the corner to gas up the truck and Jim soon became chatty friends with the owner. The service station had a rope of brightly-colored triangle flags that hung in front of his business to attract the eye.

On our way to the first open house, Jim stopped in and this nice man said, "Would you like to borrow my flags for the Open House?"

Jim thought it was a great idea, and that's one way we advertised our open houses until we could afford to buy our own flags. For that first open house, we also set out a transistor radio with music playing and a table with a lemonade jug and cookies. We were all set up and I removed my shoes to walk through the finished home while Jim stood outside. I saw our work in every detail. Jim had managed the construction and helped with as much of the labor as he could. I watched the children and kept our books, got to choose all the finishes, and when the crews cleared out, I hauled cleaning supplies in and made it sparkle. All of this was with the boys in tow. Jim washed the windows outside while I worked away on the interior. That day I thought it looked very nice—especially for the price point. It would make a good family home.

Then we waited for visitors and wrung our hands because we really could not afford to have it sit on the market. Most of the early guests were friends who wanted to be supportive and some curious neighbors. We'd have to hustle to get it sold.

After that, Jim and I alternated weekend open house dates. On Saturday I watched the two boys while Jim tended the lemonade and music. On Sunday we traded duties. The home ended up selling and from the proceeds, we budgeted ourselves an allotment to get by on until we could finish and sell another. Every two weeks, I drove to the bank in Salt Lake to make an accounting of expenses and drew down enough money from the loan to pay subcontractors. Although the boys often went to Salt Lake with me, they really suffered no major boredom with so many construction dirt piles in their lives.

The year had gone well for us, and as winter came on we looked forward to the Toronto visit postponed from the year before. Shortly before Christmas, Jim told me, "I know we said the trip would be our present, but let's go shopping. You deserve to look nice on our trip."

We got a babysitter (what a treat) and went to Samuel's Department Store on Washington Boulevard to pick out several new outfits. I got a very Scottish red plaid wool dress, a blue wool dress, and a sparkling copper cocktail dress to wear on New Year's Eve. Oh, and a slip.

When we finally arrived at Connolly Acres, all three of Jim's Robertson cousins Jimmy, Sheila, and Joan ran outside. Jim was taken aback by how grown up they were.

"Do you remember me?" Jim asked as Sheila threw her arms around him.

She responded, "Yes! We've missed you!"

The younger Jimmy added, "The year you were here was the best, but when you drove off, we didn't know if you'd ever make it back."

Jim seemed struck by the passage of time embodied in the two younger cousins—now young adults—standing before us. Jimmy was a smart, artistic young man, a future valedictorian. He agreed to babysit for us on New Year's Eve. Sheila was a spirited young wife. We were less surprised by Joan because she had stayed with us on her way to Los Angeles. It was wonderful that she could fly home for the holidays so we could all be together.

Aunt Jean made her way over and surveyed Jim. "You're even handsomer than when you left," she said. I could see they were a loving, affectionate family and she hugged Jim for as long as he could stand it.

"After you headed west in that car, I've often been reminded of that song, *The Wayward Wind*," she said after she finally let go of him.

Jim searched for words of apology, "It took a while to get on my feet. But you're my family. I will always come back." She seemed touched.

Then she turned attention to me with soft, open arms. Everything about her struck me as jolly.

"Norma! You are even prettier in person." Once inside, she showed us a wall of pictures in the dining room she had hung of our little family.

Although we were meeting for the first time, I felt as though I already knew them all. Jim's letters during his last year in school had included tidbits about their family life, we always called them on holidays, and Jim never forgot a birthday. They were on our minds more than they realized. From here on, we would make sure they knew how much we cared.

Throughout the visit, Jimmy, Sheila, and Joan recalled memories of when Jim lived there. That year had left an important mark on Jim and the cousins alike. The three cousins also doted after the boys for the entire visit. Their home was cozy with laughter, and records were always playing on the turntable. Uncle Jack had old fashioned sensibilities like Archie Bunker from the TV show, and he was funny too. One evening we went to dinner at a nice restaurant in the city and the waiter flicked a napkin. As he leaned in, Jack straightened his spine and in a blustering flurry, brushed the waiter's hands away from his lap.

Over dinner Aunt Jean said, "You two seem so good together."

Jim said, "We have big plans."

She nodded, "Of course you do. You are James E. Kier. You take after the name."

Jim said, "I feel a responsibility."

Aunt Jean turned toward me fondly, "And I can tell that you are in good hands with this little lady."

Jim said, "Norma's got grit."

Aunt Jean nodded, "She's pretty to boot." I blushed and took a sip of wine.

Aunt Jean turned toward Jack and said, "I hope the two of you will be as happy together as we've been."

He chimed in, "Cradle robber that I am."

She laughed and turned to me, "We married when I was just fifteen and he has been very good to me."

I smiled, "That's when Jim and I met, too. Sometimes it's old enough to know how you feel."

From what I could tell, I agreed with Aunt Jean; the two of them were a good match. Uncle Jack was a hard worker and would come home late to a plate of dinner warming atop a simmering kettle, like my mum used to do for my dad. Uncle Jack was a pillar during a few difficult patches when she lost weight and her skin became sallow, but in her good periods—most the time—she was an affectionate and lively partner.

A few days later was New Year's Eve and I swooshed about to get ready for a black-tie affair at Castle Loma, a real castle just outside Toronto. I emerged from their one bathroom in my evening gown and Jim whispered in my ear, "Hubba hubba." I felt like Cinderella at age 25. As we emerged to leave—just the two of us without the children for the first time in forever—Aunt Jean and Uncle Jack's party guests were trickling in.

Some men put on a little good-natured whistling, and as we kissed the children goodbye, a chorus of well-wishes sent us out the door, "Have fun!" and "Be good!"

Aunt Jean scooted over and leaned in to me, 'Darlin' you can have fun, or you can be good. But you cannot do both." I laughed and one corner of Jim's mouth turned up in that half-serious, half-mischievous grin of his.

It had been so long since we had danced all evening and it felt wonderful, then we kissed to celebrate 1961. What an eventful year it had been for us and now we were ready to usher in the future. As silver and black balloons cascaded onto the dance floor, Jim took my hand and spun me out. When I whirled back he said, "Good things are coming. I can feel it."

The band finally stopped playing and on our way back after 3 am, I said, "Gosh, I feel like inconsiderate guests. I hope we don't wake everyone."

But as we pulled in the drive, every window glowed and we could see shapes still dancing. Jim opened my door, his shoes squeaking on packed snow, and I held onto his arm for support. We heard trademark Robertson laughter and music coming from inside. Aunt Jean's floor must have had permanent wear from family members bustling to keep the turntable supplied with fresh records every night of the year. A dozen friends had drinks in hand, some playing cards, and at the room's center was Aunt Jean dancing in fuzzy blue slippers.

Uncle Jack slouched in an armchair getting forty winks, and at the sound of the door he sprang up saying, "Welcome back! Party's just getting started." He took Aunt Jean's hand and they danced for us.

The next morning, everyone but the boys wanted to sleep. Joan had to leave that morning for Los Angeles and she kissed her parents goodbye in their bed.

As the time approached for us to go home, Jim said, "We need to go see Dorothy."

His mother was still a mystery to me and I wondered what she would be like.

Jim offered no commentary, only insisting that the children stay behind at the house, "She's not very grandmotherly."

Uncle Jack drove us since they picked Dorothy up most days. After we knocked, we heard shuffling and then a long bit of fumbling with the chain before she peeked out.

"Jimmy," she said. Then we were invited to sit down in her sparse living room. She seemed to be making an effort of politeness and Jim motioned toward me.

"Do you know who this is?"

She nodded, "Yes."

He said in a loud, slow voice, "It's my wife, Norma."

She replied, "Yes."

Then I asked, "How are you feeling, Dorothy?"

The answer again was, "Yes."

Jim asked, "Do you need anything?"

"Yes." She could not articulate what that might be. She kept smoothing her hair and looking out the window while Jim fidgeted with keys.

After half an hour, he said, "Well, we must be going. You take care."

Jim patted her shoulder and I gave her a hug while saying, "It was very nice to meet you."

She nodded, "Yes."

As we parted, Jim promised Dorothy to return as soon as we could, and he always kept a promise. As we drove away, I studied his face for a hint of how he was feeling, but emotion was buried and he said nothing.

Aunt Jean and I did dishes that night. Jimmy played with the boys while Uncle Jack and Jim talked in the living room. I thought about our visit to Dorothy and how Jim seemed detached.

I asked Aunt Jean, "Was Dorothy always like this?"

Aunt Jean shook her head, "No, she used to be beautiful and fun, but then got wild."

Then I got up the nerve to ask, "Why wouldn't she ever tell Jim who his father was?"

Aunt Jean kept washing and said, "Not *wouldn't*, dear. *Couldn't*."

We left and when we promised Aunt Jean, Uncle Jack, and cousin Jimmy that we would return as soon as we could, it came from a place of genuine longing on my part as well as Jim's. In a word, family.

Then it was back to work and back on budget. I was glad that the boys were young because they knew nothing different than eating scrambled eggs and beans so often. As I put together economical meals, I was grateful for my mother who taught me to make do on so little. We also moved from home to home a lot. If a house did not sell right away, we moved in and made it look more appealing with furniture and decorations that I put together. It always sold faster that way and was worth the effort of keeping our home ready to show.

We lived close enough to the financial edge that we did everything ourselves that we could. We got into a routine when the homes were finished for Jim to do the windows outside while I cleaned the inside. I was pregnant again, but this changed very little of my routine.

One day I was feeling exhausted, but was still scrubbing away when I looked out the window where Jim was supposed to be getting the outside ready. He stood there jabbering with some building inspector, the two of them looking animated and laughing. Well, on the upside I cleaned more vigorously when I was mad, and saved up words for when we got home. One thing about our marriage, I got to have my say, and we never stayed upset for long. For one thing, there simply wasn't time for that sort of nonsense.

The pregnancy progressed as the others had and one afternoon, I was I working away as Jim's secretary in our little bedroom office, with my stomach beginning to bulge into my typing desk. My workspace was adjacent to Jim's desk, a spare door on cinderblocks.

I looked up and smiled, saying, "When you gave me typing lessons in the tenth grade, that was a pretty good investment on your part."

He half-grinned and slid into his Scottish brogue, "The Lassie married me for mah noggin, not mah gold."

We would ultimately pay that $20,000 loan within three years and after that, Jim presented Bill Wood with a multi-page plan to buy more properties and have Prudential finance them. Bill never really had to point out anywhere that we might get stretched thin because Jim's risk tolerance was probably tighter than Bill's. This made for a good partnership, and the pair would often meet over a working lunch. During this time, Bill started putting together some of his own deals outside of the day job, hiring us to do the construction.

Bill liked to joke, "I bring the dough. You do the work. It's perfect." We could see that Bill was actively working toward a time when he could be free from the skinny tie and suit he had to wear as a banker.

At home as we prepared for baby number three, Steve and Scott's Tonka Trucks did construction on our hardwood floors. I fretted about the wear and tear, but good craftsmanship holds up. When you only have one child, you take everything in with wonder and are so eager to teach them everything. With Scott, two things changed. The first was that I was content to let him pass milestones on his own time, not feeling I had to chase him into anything. The second was that I saw Steve and Scott's personalities in contrast to each other. Where Steve was demanding, Scott was relaxed and loving from the beginning and patient in his needs. He had round cheeks and an infectious giggle from day one.

Scott cupped bugs in his hands and stuffed them into pockets, enthralled with the little critters. Steve would storm in like the Tasmanian Devil and soon Scott would be hollering, "Mooooom! Mom! Steve squashed my bug."

Scott never killed anything through recklessness or dismemberment. I learned to inspect every pocket before doing laundry and to pick the linings clean of insect parts. Scott also flirted with open flame any chance he got. One day he came home with the soles of his rubber boots melted black from stomping out a campfire that came within a breath of going wild. Another time he lit the field on fire behind our home.

When Jim spotted the smoke, he took off on a dead run. I yelled, "Should I call the fire department?"

Jim hollered, "Not yet..." but after a minute yelled up at me on the deck, "Call, Norma!" By the time a truck zoomed up, they had quelled the flame and we did not get fined, but it was much too close.

As soon as Scott was big enough to go exploring, the pair would head out into the hillsides for hours or go watch the farmer do his work across the street. They trudged home at dusk. Under my nose, I always thought one would kill the other, but on their own they were the best of buddies.

One spring day, Jim was building a model home we named the Bonnie Jean in Pleasant View and I fixed a sack lunch so we could eat together. I loaded up the boys and we met Jim at the site. From the street, I admired how good the place was looking. It had reached that point when outside observers start oohing and aahing. The timeline in a construction project is funny because so much of the difficult, not-so-pretty work seems to take forever, and it doesn't look like much is happening. Planning and permits can drag on for a long time, and then there's excavation and foundation work. Finally, there's a phase when all the finishing touches come together and *then* it starts getting compliments. Painters, decorators, and masonry contractors get a lot of credit while foundation guys can feel like chopped liver.

In any case, the driveway had just been poured and I stepped out in a maternity outfit and admired the work. We parked on the street and Jim waved at us from the front door. Scott spotted his daddy and broke free at a full gallop. Jim's expletives were not quick enough to stop the little tot from making a beeline straight through the driveway. After a few feet, Scott noticed it was wet, and then he stopped to look around. This was the point when his ankles settled in. He tried to move, but the slurry swallowed his feet like quicksand and our son was stuck. Jim fished him out and hosed off his feet.

Around the same time when Steve was about four, his dad had him along at a job site. Jim needed to talk to some subs and Steve asked, "What should I play with today?"

Jim backed his truck up to a pile of damaged bricks that needed to be hauled off. "I want you to load this pile of bricks in the back of my truck. I'll be back in a few minutes."

His plan was to have him load a few bricks and after he was done talking, they would push the bricks back into the pile and be on their way. Well, Jim got carried away and never did have that sense when mothers tune into to a child who has been quiet too long. He might have been alarmed for this reason, but he came out to the truck, and the entire pile was loaded. The bed was heaping with bricks, the axles practically touched dirt, and two tires were flat. He looked at his watch, wondering how long exactly had passed. What to do?

He patted Steve on the head and said, "Well done, son. Now let's unload them!" They then emptied the truck together, fixed the tires, and headed out.

My pregnancy was far along by now and juggling everything had made the time go quickly. Jim came into our 10x10 spare-bedroom office where I was tapping away at my little typewriter desk adjacent to his horizontal door/desk. He had a client with him, so I scooted my chair to make room. Now I realized that the few square inches that had been added to my tummy had made the space too small for this arrangement. I offered to bring in some lemonade, and then waited until our guest left before returning to my work. The next time I heard Jim's footsteps approach with someone else, I would have to excuse myself *before* they entered and it got awkward.

That night before bed, Jim told me, "After this baby comes, I'll get working on the basement." I breathed relief. The baby could stay in a bassinet by us for a while, but we'd need another room in time. Building a bigger office downstairs would also separate work from home-life by a set of stairs. One thing about Jim, he could lose certain details, but I never had to ask him to take care of big projects like this. He saw what needed to be done and got to it.

I had noticed another gradual change during this pregnancy. He had begun taking on part of the housework, doing the dishes and other odd jobs. It relieved my burden a great deal and I was quick to express gratitude and reinforce what he was doing.

Maybe it sounds trite, but it seemed like the world was changing around us. Jim picked up on it and changed, too. When we first married in the 50s, duties of men and women seemed clearly delineated. In our marriage, though, we had been full partners in business. I took on many extra duties that most housewives did not have to worry about. Nevertheless, I loved our life and I told Jim many times, "I am so glad you chose construction as your life's work because it means I can be in it with you." I felt appreciated and needed, even if I sometimes noticed an imbalance in workload. I generally kept quiet because Jim was truly a very hard worker, but little-by-little, I saw changes. Our workloads evened out.

On the evening of May 12, 1964, labor came on hard and we went into the drill. We called a neighbor who had her own large family and had offered to stay with our boys. After we left, she slipped into our bed and went to sleep. It was another clockwork delivery, and at 8:30 a.m. the doctor handed me a perfect child and said, "Congratulations, Norma. She's a girl." She weighed 7 pounds, 10 ounces.

Absolute joy radiated from my heart, onto my cheeks, and into every finger and toe. We had a third child, a beautiful daughter with a lot of hair. A girl would join me in my activities. Jim was just as elated as I, if that's possible.

We had a list of names, and I had put one on the list that I just loved even though we had already used it for one of our model homes: the Bonnie Jean. We had a Scottish theme in our marketing and this one fit the company. I suppose it is a true construction family when your daughter is named after a model home.

When we called the boys and told them we had a girl, they may have said, "Ick! A *girl.*" When we brought her home, that changed and they kissed her so much I had to remind them how tiny she was. When she became big enough, she was everywhere they were, although they also teased her incessantly.

Mum and Dad came down to help as they had done with the boys. What a Godsend they were. Mum and I even got away just the two of us, leaving the kids with Jim. Sometimes when we returned, though, Jim would have a slightly cagey look and say, "Everything's fine here!" I had to wonder what may have happened while we were gone, but the kids did seem fine.

The boys adored their grandparents, and I always cried when they drove away. I couldn't help thinking that every time you leave a loved one, it could be the last time.

I had decorated the boys' room in a cowboy theme with western style bunk beds and a little table and chairs in the corner. There was no door, just a beaded curtain, which helped me keep watch on their antics. When clients came to the house to choose decor, I'd sit the boys down at that little table with crayons and say, "Now color, please." Bonnie sat in a bouncer and whenever she was near the boys, she was as happy as a lark.

Jim scrambled to finish the basement by the time Bonnie was out of a bassinet so she could move into her own room. We got a new office in the finished basement, and now also had a family room where the kids could play. The extra square feet made an enormous difference in our living situation.

When Bonnie was still just a baby, we took our family on a trip to Toronto to see Aunt Jean and Uncle Jack. While there, we looked up our old friend Freddie Goodfellow who we hadn't seen in many years. We met him and his wife for dinner in Toronto and the political banter fired up between Jim and Freddie like no time at all had passed. Freddie was in good form, although he had become agitated with Canada's politics. Now the skin graft scars around his nose from his crash gave the right amount of character to an otherwise smooth face. Over the entrée he announced, "We've finally had enough. Come Christmas we're moving to Australia."

That winter, I sent our last Christmas card to their address in Canada, always including them on our ever-growing list. On big holidays I always took the opportunity to send a card or flowers to Dorothy, too. When they drove across the continent to catch a boat to Australia, Freddie's family stayed with us for a single night. They had packed the family and a few belongings into an English car about the size of a Volkswagen Beetle. It reminded me of how my family had piled into a car like it when we lived in Wainwright. We had a wonderful visit catching up. Somehow with Freddie it always felt as though no time had passed, and Jim seemed boyish in his presence.

Sometime later, we received word that Freddie had survived the second plane crash of his life while flying over the outback with the Australian Air Force. It would leave him a paraplegic, but with no less zest. He was two lives down, but after initial recovery still lived to the fullest and enrolled in law school.

Our routine continued with three children running circles around me. My daily tasks included a bank run to Commercial Security on 25th and Washington Boulevard. One day while working with the teller, I had Bonnie on my hip while Steve stood by my side. Scott kept tugging at my pants.

"Be patient," I said and then turned to give a signature. When I glanced back down, panic washed over me, "Where's Scott?" I panned the lobby and spotted him descending the escalator with a nice gentleman. He had a collected look, like a mini businessman.

That year we began the annual school-shopping trip for Steve, which would also outfit Scott in new clothes. We trekked to JC Penny downtown where I purchased five pairs of jeans and five shirts for each. Like in the bank earlier, I turned around in frantic fear after noticing Scott missing.

As we searched underneath racks and in dressing room corridors, a tinny sounding P.A. system interrupted the music track, "Will the mother of Scott Kier please come to the service desk?" He had become lost wandering in his own little world until someone noticed him. I jogged to the front of the store and gave him a big hug. I can't count how many times that scene repeated.

When Bonnie was a toddler, she liked to fish my panties out of the drawer and put them on her head. I was in the office talking with a salesman I had never met before, and in she waddled wearing a diaper on her bottom and my underwear on her head. I flushed red, shooed her out of the room, and tried to act like nothing happened.

While we still lived in North Ogden, Steve was about seven and had eyed the price of penny candy in the store. He roughly calculated the mountain of candy he could buy with a week's worth of lunch money. One day after getting his dollar bill, he invited his buddies on a shopping spree, following which they gorged themselves on treats. The next day, he returned from school ravenous for a snack, and the next morning I saw him at the fridge putting an apple and bread into his backpack. When he got home, he went straight for the fridge. On day three, I met him at the refrigerator and asked why he was so hungry. He shrugged, but his eyes shifted and he was given away.

I pressed him. "Have you been eating lunch?" He nodded yes, but looked at his shoes.

"What did you do with your lunch money?" I could tell he was considering a far-fetched story that might involve dogs or Scott, but I stopped him, "It will be much worse if you lie."

I studied his face and finally he spilled the beans. When Jim came home, I explained the situation in front of Steve and then said that his father and I would discuss how he could make amends.

A little while later, we walked out together and announced, "For the next two weekends you will be sweeping out houses to pay us back for your lunch money." Despite some goofing off, that kid did a good job.

Steve had always been a tease with Scott, and by this time the two boys often teamed up to invent mischief that would get a rise out of their sister. She had a stuffed bear, and I later learned that when I wasn't around, a favorite pastime was tossing it back and forth, farther and farther, punching it in between until they got Bonnie in tears.

In early elementary school, Steve asked me to be a room mother and, busy as life was, I said yes. The day might come when the kids would not want their mother around their friends. The elementary school in North Ogden had a big Halloween festival every year and they asked the room mothers to each decorate a booth with a game in it. Well, this was one time when being a working mother in a family construction business came in handy. I recruited two of our carpenters to build a sturdy wooden storefront with a large black cat out front. Kids would win a prize if they could toss a loop and ring its tail. It turned out so cute all brightly painted. The boys were pleased at their well-constructed booth next to the others which were also very cute, but made of cardboard and decorated with craft supplies.

One of the other mothers said something like, "Well yours certainly is an *achievement*."

I tried to downplay it, but the school used it for many years and I think we all took small pride in building something to last.

STAY OR GO?

———————◼———————

By 1969, Steve was eleven, Scott was nine, and Bonnie was five. We had been carving out an existence and moving from home to home, but honestly, it was quite a struggle still. We worked very, very hard but barely had enough left over for groceries. Our family's finances aside, the biggest external threat to a construction company is the economy, which can turn the whole industry on its head in a blink. The country had slumped into the throes of a full-blown recession, and the Federal Reserve had been steadily raising interest rates, a death knell to the already sputtering construction industry. The country was entering an era of skyrocketing inflation.

With Bonnie about to enter Kindergarten, part of me dreaded the idea of our youngest getting so big, while the other part felt relieved to start working full-time with Jim. If I could do more with the business, it might open the pressure valve.

Then a monkey wrench: I showed unmistakable signs of pregnancy. We had not planned for this contingency. Our family had felt complete with three children. It was a good number for us and we were ready to focus on work. Of course I knew we knew we would be joyful at having another child join our family, but I had to find the words to tell Jim. I somehow did, although this change of plans took some getting used to.

Being pregnant made everyday fiascos feel a little harder. We were almost ready to showcase in the Parade of Homes, when Steve tormented Scott until he chucked a rock at his brother on the job site. It hit the mark and made a nasty gash. Jim rushed Steve in for stitches and made the perpetrator watch, hoping it would teach consequences.

We took the opportunity while I was still feeling energetic at about five months to take the kids on a camping trip to Banff. I was not yet relegated to maternity wear, just loose clothing and pants with stretchy waistbands. It was a good time to camp, and I wasn't too uncomfortable to sleep in a tent. I had certainly done it before.

To fund the trip, I saved up S&H green stamps in little coupon books, a sort of rewards program that grocery stores and gas stations offered, to be redeemed for merchandise. During those years, the S&H reward catalog was the largest publication in America and it was reported that there were three times as many green stamps as U.S. postage stamps printed at the time. We had decided to redeem ours for a barbecue and other equipment, an investment we could use for years. We also rented a big tent from Tent and Awning out of Salt Lake, crammed the station wagon full, and off we went.

Our first night in the Glacier National Park was in spectacular, lush country with craggy mountains, waterfalls, clear cold lakes, and tall fragrant conifers: cedars and hemlock trees. We soaked in the broad expanses of unspoiled Montana wilderness all around. After the drive, we were all anxious to get out and explore, but darkness fell before there was much time. Instead we fixed dinner, played charades around the fire, and retired to the tent.

Then we drove to the Banff area and made camp again as it began to rain. It came down all night. The sturdy tent stayed dry and the kids got a kick out of hearing fat droplets pepper the canvas roof. The next morning, we unzipped the flaps to peek out. We saw gray skies and drizzle in all directions and it seemed that the sun had timed a holiday just in time for ours. Jim and the kids suited up for exploring and before long, their feet were mud-soaked stumps with denim pant legs completely coated in gooey muck. It clung to everything and then pine needles stuck to the mud. We peeled off wet layers and hung them inside the tent's vestibule. We had packed plenty of extra clothes, but it had taken only minutes to soak through one outfit.

We hunkered down—still cheerfully—to entertain ourselves with games and coloring books inside. "Look how much worse it could be," I said, "The tent is dry, we're healthy, and we are in this beautiful place."

We kept the kids entertained as long as we could before venturing out to soak through another set of clothes at dinnertime. We kept a fire on life support before it let off a dying gasp of steam and gave up the ghost.

On night two, the sound of rain on the tent had less novelty, and by night three we went to sleep in our last dry threads. At about two o'clock a.m. Jim nudged me.

"Norma. The tent is flooded," he said. I rubbed my eyes and patted my hands into little puddles all about. A canvas tent just stops trying after a while. We roused Steve first, who elbowed Scott, who kneed Bonnie. We donned damp jackets, put on squishy shoes, and broke camp. Everyone piled in, and I wondered if the car would ever get clean again. Then we drove into Banff for a motel and I looked on the bright side again, "Now we get to stay in a motel!"

The next morning we tracked down a laundromat, washing all our muddy clothes with our canvas tent's metal grommets clanging around and around in dryers. We killed time by perusing a rack of tourist brochures offering adventures we could not have in the rain. When we removed warm clothes from the dryer, the fabric softener smelled heavenly. When I put on my pants, though, I wondered if they had shrunk. They felt so uncomfortable I had a hard time wanting to eat— they constricted my pregnant middle and made me feel full.

The weather never broke. We spent that entire trip in a spectacular place either rain-soaked or stuck inside, which made the drive home feel much longer than usual. Three restless children fought in the backseat for nothing better to do. I shifted in the passenger seat.

"Gosh it feels like the baby is just as cooped up as we are!" It was nonstop movement, an order of magnitude more than with the other three pregnancies.

When we got home, I studied the mirror. I looked like I was having an elephant! We had a little junk food on the trip but I may have actually eaten less because I was so uncomfortable at mealtime. I always felt full.

When I went in for the next pre-natal appointment, my regular doctor was on vacation so I saw a substitute.

After he weighed me, I joked, "Maybe I ate too much on our trip!"

His eyes gave me the up-and-down and he said, "Wouldn't hurt to watch it."

That wounded me a bit, so I asked very tentatively, voicing words for the first time, "Could I be having twins?" He raised an eyebrow as if he'd heard that one a hundred times when women were shocked at weight gain.

"We can't do an x-ray until seven months. So for now, just follow this diet." He sent me on my merry way with a handout advising me to eat more celery and go easy on the ice cream.

At lunchtime following the appointment, I forced myself to get down my usual pregnancy meal: a hard-boiled egg, an apple, and a piece of toast. It took some discipline to eat all of it. After that, I stole a minute in front of the mirror, frowning. Then I turned to the side and frowned even more. My tummy bulged straight out. Finally, I pivoted and caught the view from behind where you couldn't even tell I was pregnant. I told the mirror, "There, that's not so bad," and crumpled up the diet paper.

I took Bonnie to the seven-month appointment with my regular doctor and when the x-ray image came back, even Bonnie could see one baby situated on top with another snuggled in below. My doctor was very kind. His first concern was how a five-foot, 98 pounder could carry twins, so he gave me some orders.

The first was bed rest, which he emphasized by saying, "If you deliver early, just think of the cost of two babies in incubators."

Given our financial situation, this was sobering. Truly, though, the idea of lying around was a pipe dream. The second order was that Jim was to mix me a single cocktail every evening to slow labor. Now that lifted my spirits. Finally, the doctor announced that he would be visiting me at home for the remainder of my pregnancy. Unbelievably nice!

Bonnie was so tickled at the idea of twins and I wondered how long I had already known it. Had I known it back when I bought twin insurance with my first pregnancy? It was daunting news, but part of me was also excited. Twins were special indeed.

I took a deep breath and thought through ways to break this development to Jim. "Bonnie, sweetheart, will you please let me tell Daddy about the twins myself?"

She looked up, always one to take an assignment seriously, "Okay, Mum."

There was no good way to say, "There was news at the doctor today." Long pause.

"The x-ray explained why I'm so huge. There are two babies." Jim looked at me, blinked hard as if to hold back regrettable words, and walked out of the room. We stewed in silence for a day, I think both of us blaming the other in the absurd way that only married couples would understand, "You did this," as the other thinks, "No YOU did this."

By the next day, Jim had thawed, "What exactly did the doctor say? Give me the facts."

He tugged at his ear as I explained, "The babies both look healthy, but twins are a higher risk for premature labor so I can't over-do it." He expected as much, but I kept the full bed rest lecture to myself. It was out of the question so there was no use adding that to Jim's list of concerns.

"Oh, and he suggested that you make me a cocktail each evening to slow labor."

Jim smiled, "You put him up to that."

I smiled back, "That is the God's honest truth." So Jim walked in the other room and returned with a fruity drink in a sweating lowball glass.

Jim met Bill Wood for a Friday lunch at *The Horse*, a private club where we had a membership. The walls were paneled with faux half-timber stable doors that reached shoulder height, and burlap paneling to the ceiling. Neon signs and tiffany shades lit the room here and there, and wood beams spanned the ceiling. A big sign read, "You can't drink all day if you don't start in the morning."

Bill had grown his hair out and wore it in a ponytail like the hippies in California. They plopped into chairs as if weighted by the workweek as Bill asked, "How's the little mama?"

Jim grimaced, "Norma is having twins."

Bill grinned, "Copasetic. Your own Doublemint commercial."

After a drink, Jim relaxed and opened up, "If business doesn't improve, we might have to go back to Canada."

Bill seemed unfazed, as always, "Hold your horses. Something will pan out."

Jim was skeptical and Bill got philosophical, "Lady luck favors the prepared, my friend."

Then Bill added, "Nobody works harder than you, so don't freak out. Your ship will come in." Then Bill added another thought, "Can I give you a piece of advice as a friend? After those babies come, ratchet it back. It's a real drag to miss time with your kids." Bill had been divorced and knew what it was to split time with his children.

With our news, we reconsidered our living arrangements because in an instant, our family situation went from average to large. Now we contemplated a spec home we were building across from the Emerald Hills subdivision in South Ogden. Before the day was up, we had drawn several modifications. Soon our home in North Ogden was on the market and at seven months pregnant with twins, we were moving.

Aunt Jean and Uncle Jack came to see us and we were delighted that their good humor filled our home before life changed with twins. They came as often as they could and generally stayed for about three weeks, calling our place "The Kier Hotel." Having extra hands was also a great help as we completed construction and moved in while ignoring bed rest.

Uncle Jack was also great with our kids, playing house with Bonnie and roughhousing with the boys. One evening after dinner, Jack sat at the dinner table as Aunt Jean and I tried to pass in the hallway. When her jolly plumpness brushed against my overgrown stomach, he called out, "Watch out, you'll get stuck!"

Steve was now in Little League football and I would not miss a game for anything. During a nail-biting play, I was cheering like a mad woman and one of the kids in the huddle with Steve asked, "Whose mom was that, anyway?"

Steve shrugged, "No idea." Later he was running to the ball with other guys coming after him and I leaped to the sidelines and scurried alongside while scooping up my enormous belly for support.

"Run!" I shouted.

I heard a child behind me say, "Hey will you look at that fat lady!" Adults had concerned looks, as if I might go into labor on the spot.

Whenever I had to walk up the stairs, Scott came running to take my hand and guide me up; he was such a little gentleman. I accepted his help and took care not to trip. I thought, "If I fall on this little man, I will squash him."

By the eighth month, I was terribly big and uncomfortable with my stomach sticking straight out. It had become hard as a basketball. At this point I was forced to get off my feet, at least some of the time. I calculated payroll and wrote checks by hand from bed. I invited couples in to choose colors bedside. I was getting more miserable by the day. One night, Bonnie came into our room where I lay sprawled on the bed with my head over backward to get comfortable. I hefted myself up—not a small undertaking—when I saw she was sniffling from carpet-burned forearms. The boys had been pulling her around the living room, after which they punched the lights out of her teddy bear. She came in to announce, "If the twins are boys I am leaving home."

Twice I had strong enough pains that we went to the hospital. With such quick labor every other time, Jim did not want to chance twins being born in the car. With three weeks to go, the doctor visited and told me that the babies had each reached five pounds and I could start moving again. I never confessed how much I had still done throughout. Nesting urges set in and I vacuumed like crazy for the next week. Maybe it will put me into labor, I hoped.

With two weeks to due date, I talked to Mum who said, "Your brother Jon was late so I took castor oil and it worked like a charm." The next afternoon, I sent Jim to the pharmacy and I poured two bottles into orange juice and inspected the repulsive globules. One, two, three, go.

That evening, for the third time, labor pains set in. And hard. I lumbered to the car with as much hurry as I had in me. Jim put pedal to the metal and screeched into the emergency entrance. He opened my door and I tried to get up, but I couldn't move even with his help. The first baby was already coming. Jim rushed inside and an E.R. team ran out with a stretcher then got me onto it.

They tried putting me on my back but I gasped, "I can't," and rolled onto my side instead. Bright lights blurred as they jostled me down the hallway, and I spotted a doctor running and tying his gown on the move.

A nurse yelled at him, "Doctor, she's heading! She's heading!" They shooed Jim into the waiting area, tore around a corner, and we slid into the delivery room. The doctor was just catching up.

He too tried to roll me over. "I...can't lay...on my back," I pushed the words out between hard contractions and spouts of air.

"It's okay. Just breathe," he said and put my feet in the stirrups sideways. "They used this position in the old days." I grimaced at another fierce contraction and he said, "Hang in there. This will go quick." With no time for them to do anything about the pain, a fireball shot through my body and our first twin pushed her way into the world. The nurse dotted sweat from my head and I took a breath.

The doctor gave his pronouncement, "A girl and she's perfect." Hooray! The entire room exhaled as he dabbed her squirming little body with a towel then handed her to me. My body relaxed for a minute as intervals between contractions lengthened.

We got acquainted and I said, "A girl! Bonnie won't leave home now."

A nurse smiled, "She's plump for a twin," then added, "About six pounds." We named this first baby Kara.

They let me hold her for a lovely but too-brief moment before whisking her away. "You have more work to do," the doctor said. "Ready?" I nodded but when I went to push, it was like I could not get hold, as if our second baby was missing. I went white.

"I can't feel the baby."

The doctor said, "Push again, push again." But I could not grip anything. My stomach felt deflated and empty. I felt nothing in there. His hand reassured my shoulder as he crouched forward to listen with his stethoscope, ordering, "Shhhh!"

I held my breath without realizing it and he stood up satisfied, "There is movement. Keep going. It's just not so crowded in there now." Contractions resumed but without the same urgency as before. They gave me something for the pain this time before I was to concentrate on bearing down again. Thirteen minutes felt like a very long time after the first baby, but finally the doctor coaxed our second twin—Kimi—into the world.

"Congratulations. You have two beautiful baby girls." I felt a rush of happiness that I cannot put into words. I beamed and cried tears of joy, holding the second wiggling infant who was also nearly six pounds and healthy. They were both beautiful infants, and it felt like far more than twice the joy, a transcendent experience that I cannot put into words.

I felt the room right itself. None of us had time before to think how tense the scene had been minutes earlier. It was a high-risk delivery and now the room was bursting with celebration as they ushered Jim into the room. They handed him our second little girl to hold as the doctor said, "This is quite a wife you have."

Jim nodded, "She sure is."

That was November 5, 1969. When we phoned the news home to the boys, Steve and Scott flew onto the back deck and called to their friends playing in the subdivision below, "The twins are here! The twins are here!" News spread fast that way.

My room was across from the nursery and while I rested I could hear two little grannies talking outside my door.

"Oh my goodness! Would you look at those beautiful twins?"

The other replied, "Yes, and have you seen the tiny mother?" There had been over twelve pounds of babies plus fluid in my small frame.

Jim had gone home now and it was time to sleep. Although my body was spent, I could not quiet my mind from a mix of elation and worry. Uncertainty enveloped me as I wondered how we would manage. The business was struggling. Secretarial work had piled up and I shuddered at how much backlog awaited. Newborn twins might demand more than I had to give, and I had three others to love, too. My mind spun on a loop until a nurse came in with a sleeping pill. For the first time in ages, I slept deeply.

A normal hospital stay was three days for a single baby and that is exactly when we left with Kara and Kimi. I felt blessed for how perfect these girls were and I looked forward to taking our babies home, even though it meant facing life without hospital staff to help.

On the way home, Jim said, "I need to swing by the lumber store."

I nodded but fired off a warning, "Don't get chatty." I tended to our babies in the back while he tended business inside. I brushed it off and reminded myself, "It could be worse. At least he isn't lazy."

My mum and dad came down not long after we went home. We put our original crib in their room and another secondhand one in ours. Jim returned to work and I tried to talk myself into a better attitude, but within a few days, I had the usual dump of hormones. After a full-body cry, I slept and woke up feeling better. I had puffy eyes and Mum gave me a knowing hug without dispensing advice or platitudes.

I was reminded that none of my hardships compared to her life. She would never have two pennies in the bank and although I loved my dad, I could not have been married to him. She also carried responsibility for her youngest child, Bob, until the day she died.

In those days, twins were a rarity and we got used to attention everywhere we went. We had so many visitors and Bonnie would run to the door and say, "Come see *my* twins!" There was a long haze when days and nights blurred together. It felt with the twins that the joys were exponentially greater, but some of the logistics were that much harder, too. It is a tall order to synchronize two newborn schedules.

At only five, Bonnie was a tremendous help, a natural little mother. She'd run into the other room for a diaper and baby powder when I was holding the twins. In the evening, the two of us would watch Engelbert Humperdinck, each feeding one baby. She went with me everywhere, entertaining herself for hours in apartments while I chose colors and went about decorating. Before I became an official carpet dealer, she made many trips to Salt Lake City with me to pick flooring. She also played with dolls or colored in newly finished homes and apartment units as I cleaned and prepared them for families to move in.

We had the twins baptized in our church, Trinity Presbyterian where all the others except Scott had been baptized. His baptism was in First Presbyterian where we attended for a short time after moving out of the neighborhood. Jim wore a dark navy blue suit, and I had on a skirt with jacket ensemble in the same hue. When it came time in the service, the boys stood like they were going to take their girls up, and we had a bit of wrangling to get the twins out of their arms. On the way back to our pew, I looked down and both Jim and I had throw-up down the fronts of our blue outfits. I tried dabbing it off with a rag before the service ended and our friends came up to congratulate us, but the residue remained. Perhaps navy was not the best color choice. The twins had reflux for the first year and we should have known better.

I itched to get the green-light for exercise at my six-week checkup and knew I would feel more resilient then. After I dressed and the doctor was wrapping up instructions, he had been silent about exercise.

Like a puppy, I finally jumped up to ask, "So I'm clear to work out?"

He waved his hand downward and said, "Not so fast. You have strained muscles in your stomach. Go easy on yourself and don't expect your tummy to ever be the same again."

I stood and turned quickly. Silly, stupid tears. The rest of the day I attempted a brave face, but my bottom lip quivered every time I thought about it. It felt like the doctor had canceled Christmas. It wasn't important, I knew. I told myself to be grateful for an uncomplicated pregnancy, for healthy beautiful twins, and a lovely family, for all of it.

I pulled myself together before Jim came through the door, but when he asked about my appointment it opened the release valve. I blubbered into a full-blown meltdown.

He looked unsteady and pale, then asked "Are you pregnant again?"

I wiped my nose. "Heavens no! It's silly. The doctor said I can't work out yet. And I might not get my stomach back."

Jim looked chipper, like Christmas was back on, "You look great, you know that?" We broke into laughter. It's funny how much that moment brightened my outlook.

One evening Jim settled in to unwind with a Star Trek episode. He motioned for me to sit with him, but I mumbled "I'm busy!" into a stack of laundry balanced on outstretched arms like the leaning tower of Pisa.

He shouted, "For God's sake woman! Would you sit down for once!"

I dropped the clothes and put a hand on my hip, "Right, mister stop-at-the-lumber-store-on-the-way-from-the-hospital!"

We went back and forth then left off with "You are so stubborn!" and "*I am stubborn?* Look in the mirror!" We dropped it for the time being. Before bed, we were both simmering, but kissed goodnight anyway.

The next day, Jim slipped me a greeting card that was surprisingly tender for such a strong man, and below the poem he wrote, "Let's find time to be us again." We both softened. That next night he moved the dresser in front of our bedroom door, a signal we needed privacy.

Jim went on a mission to shore up our business and when he gets like that, he has more tenacity than anyone I know. He scouted for opportunities in books about the construction business and real estate markets. My head went to sleep within seconds of crawling in bed, but Jim stayed up and read, like a hunter tracking game. He seemed to sense that at some moment, an idea would emerge like a stag from the woods.

He made time to have lunch with colleagues and watched over his friends and family like a border collie, herding everyone together. Case in point. I overheard him on the phone with a subcontractor.

" I think your bid is off. I suggest you double check the figures." Jim could not reveal whether the number was too high or low, but he would not let a friend lose his shirt because of an honest error.

In the spirit of considering all options, Jim suggested that it might be time to return to Canada. Perhaps our situation would improve back "in God's country," as Dad reminded us every time he visited. Jim reached out to city officials in Edmonton and scheduled a visit in March.

One spring evening, a windstorm came howling over the mountaintops and out of the canyons. While lying in bed, we heard garbage cans bounce clankety clank down the street. We did not get much sleep as tree limbs snapped. The next morning, the news reported wind gusts of up to 88 miles per hour, destroying mobile homes and overturning railroad cars. In our neighborhood, shingles and branches littered the streets and Jim headed out to inspect our job sites. We only sustained minor damage, but he still paid our insurance agent a visit the next morning. He left a stack of business cards.

Three weeks later, Jim and I flew to Edmonton, leaving the kids with a young couple. Our plane landed in full-on Alberta winter. Had we gone soft or what! We met with council members and sketched out a plan that told us it would indeed be feasible to relocate. We felt ambivalent. We loved Canada, but returning home felt like retreat now.

With minds not made up, we pulled back into Ogden from the airport. It was one of those sparkling clean days after a spring rain when the valley is green, the sky is robin-egg blue, and the color of snow on the mountain peaks has faded from a crisp white into a fast-melting gray. It's the kind of day when the buds are about to sprout open and announce that anything is possible. Driving through our neighborhood, we realized that this community felt like home now. Somehow Edmonton, where winter was so cold, did not.

That night over a casserole, Jim set down his fork and said, "Let's stay. We'll just work hard and think of something." I felt relief that I had not realized would be there. I had been praying to know what to do, and this felt like an answer.

FAMILY LIFE

When we returned home, we collected our messages, and it was a big stack. The business cards Jim had brought to the insurance company were now bearing fruit. Whenever a homeowner had called to make a claim, our agent recommended Kier Construction. All at once, our crews were booked for months doing roof and carport repairs, all referrals.

In retrospect, I think that difficult times and tough decisions have a way of testing how much you really want your dreams. Until we visited Edmonton, we had always held open the possibility of someday returning to mother Canada. That big, beautiful country would always be beloved by us, but perhaps it took that moment to cement that now we had two homes: one north of the border and a new one in Ogden.

Now with all the new work, some things would have to change.

Jim said, "Either you've got to get help with the twins, or I need to hire a secretary." I was adamant about remaining part of the business, so we hired childcare and shortly after that some secretarial help too since I was out decorating most of the time.

Jim kept studying for opportunities to diversify. Construction is cyclical, and to build a business for the duration, we needed more than just residential and commercial construction. But what?

One night at bedtime, Jim set down a book and said, "Apartments."

I opened my eyes, "Huh?"

He went on as I tried to come to, "Apartments are counter-cyclical. When people aren't buying homes, they move into apartments. This could help us weather any storm. And in rentals, we're building equity."

Now he went looking for where the biggest rental needs were. He studied national trends to see where Utah might be headed and scoped out the government sector. He picked apart demographic reports and chatted up experts. Utah had a shortage of affordable housing and some new programs were coming out. He saw the market going this way, and thought we could differentiate ourselves in this undefended market.

We also liked how subsidized housing helped people. Our life's work would always be to build a home where good people could begin their day with a smile, where love and family were protected. Whether it was a young family's first house, or a comfortable apartment for seniors, this purpose always remained in the forefront for us.

Government deals were also complex and Jim got jazzed about the challenge. Jim checked with contacts at the FHA office in Salt Lake who had approved many of our residential jobs. One day he got a call from an FHA associate. "A guy owns this complex in Brigham City and wants to renovate it into subsidized units. He needs a builder. Interested?"

We jumped into Jim's truck to look and he glanced at my strappy heels, "You're wearing those?"

I shrugged, "It's not a construction site yet," and Jim let it go. He probably did not want to alarm me.

As we approached, some loitering teens stared at us, as if to guard their nighttime hangout. The parking lot had weeds sprouting from cracks, and I think I could smell the place before opening the car door. We picked our way through broken glass and concrete chunks.

Threadbare carpet in the hallway gave off an odor of urine and parties. More recent tenants had left a housewarming gift, soiled diapers in the corner. We snaked our way down to the laundry room where I half covered my eyes, "This looks like a murder scene."

Jim laughed and said, "It reeks with potential, right? It needs work, and work is what we do."

The economics were right and we submitted an application to HUD that may have deforested a small country. Then we waited.

We made a trip to Canada around this time, and Jim went up ahead of time to check on a business deal in Washington state (which ended up not working out). This left me to take all five kids by plane. The twins were just nine months old and I was anxious about the flight without help. Before leaving, I gave the children a lecture and a request.

"Steve and Scott, in your father's absence, will you step up?" We jostled our caravan onto the plane and I felt judging eyes on us. I thought I heard someone say, "Oh no."

Steve and Scott, who were eleven and nine, sat in the row in front of us with Kara between them. Bonnie and I had Kimi between us. Steve and Scott fed, burped and held her like pros, and I overheard two grannies, "Would you look at those boys take care of that baby!" There was scarcely a peep out of the twins. As we exited, the pilot and flight attendant marched over like they had business and I thought, *oh boy*.

The pilot spoke, "On behalf of this airline, we would like to congratulate you on five very well-behaved children." I had never been prouder of my family, and felt a little smug at the doubters. *So there!*

Days with my parents were precious and the boys particularly enjoyed being with my dad. They were entranced by his war stories. He had a shop in the basement that he always kept neat and orderly—like he ran his office and our family—and the boys would hang out with him there. It didn't hurt that they were athletic Jessimans. Mum baked for days and spoiled us with cookies and cake.

While there, we gave our old friends Jenny and Bob Ross a call since they had moved to the Vancouver area, and it felt like old times. As an added bonus, we liked their home so much that Bob got the plans for us. We built two homes after it in Layton and South Ogden, which we called The Thunderbird, a beautiful plan.

After the kids and I got back, I received a long-distance call from Denver. HUD had approved the project! I phoned Jim, and he instructed me to send a telegram agreeing to the terms.

We always had some homes under construction and the Brigham City project revved up fast. This meant we had a steady stream of contractors in and out of our home office, so even dinnertime was hectic. We would just sit down and the doorbell would ring. I was forever after the kids to pick up their toys because our home was an example of our work. The dog barking sometimes set off a mad dash to shove the last clutter into closets. If our clients had ever opened the wrong door, they might have been killed by falling objects.

While the business was growing fast at this time, so were the kids. The character of our company was taking shape, just as the personalities of our kids were emerging as distinct from each other.

Kara was assertive and confident from day one while Kimi was mild-mannered and patient, yet seemed born with a great sense of humor. Fiercely loyal to each other, if I ever reprimanded one, the other would come to her defense. They were playful by nature and stood out in every sense except size. If one ever got picked on at school, the other intervened. One time Kara got sent home for kicking some boys who were giving Kimi a hard time, and Jim high-fived her.

I rather enjoyed how people fawned over our twins and I could never have predicted the moment I got pregnant what fun those little girls would bring into our lives.

Bonnie naturally fell into a role as my right-hand pal, perhaps as the eldest girl, or maybe also because she didn't have a natural sibling pair like the boys or the twins.

Steve and Scott had the same group of friends, but at home still pounded on each other like bitter enemies. One day Steve was needling his brother and I'd had it. I picked up a wooden chair and whacked him. He spun around half stunned and half amused at his pint-sized mother coming after him with a chair. His mum was tougher than he thought and I never had to use the chair again.

One evening after running back and forth from the Brigham City project, it was time to shuttle the older kids to their athletic activities. We believed that sports are important to build bodies and keep kids too busy for troublemaking. It can be exhausting for parents, though, and I still had dinner to prepare. I decided on stir-fry and plopped all the vegetables on a cutting board next to a glass bowl for each. Then it was time to run Bonnie to gymnastics and I remembered my dad's voice. "All I am is a (bleepity) taxi driver."

After dropping her off, I jerked the gear into park, ran to the kitchen to peel carrots and then it was chop, chop, chop. Look at the time!

"Steve, Scott, let's go!" I herded them into the station wagon along with their gear. I deposited Steve at a pre-season football meeting and Scott at baseball practice.

On Scott's way out he asked, "Mom, I need a hat."

I smiled, "Okay, sweetie," and tacked a mental note onto my list.

When I got back to the house, I thought, "I should just leave the car idling!" I ran into the house to chop some more, then left again to pick up Bonnie. My plan was working. By the time everyone finally convened, I could throw it in a sizzling wok and voila! Ten minutes later we'd be eating a fast, healthy stir-fry. Mother of the year stuff.

Back at home, the boys dumped their equipment and I hollered, "Put your things away!"

Bonnie was setting the silverware and glasses on the table and I called to Bonnie, "Go get your brothers."

She ran to the door and yelled "Steve the Peeve and Scott the Pot!" They came running after her but she was untouchable while helping me get the meal on. The girl had brains.

Then I heard an enormous crash in the kitchen. I froze, fearing someone hurt and Jim hurtled into the kitchen. I found Bonnie crouched on the countertop, boxed in by shards on the tile. The contents of my bowls had scattered like marbles among the wreckage.

Through a quivering bottom lip she managed, "I came in for the glasses and knocked one down." It had created a chain reaction. Jim looked at Bonnie and then at me. We were both about to cry.

He announced, "Everybody in the car! Dinner is at a restaurant tonight." I felt considerably better.

We took our time over pasta, enjoying each other and a break from the ringing doorbell and telephone.

One of the boys teased Bonnie, "If you've gotta break something, let it be vegetables."

I pelted him with a napkin and laughed, "See how much worse it could be?"

That weekend, a sunny day drenched the bleachers with springtime for Scott's first baseball game. What an excited young boy, ready to get bright-white pants dirty, imagining sliding onto base and all the good stuff. He took position and as the sun burned off the morning's coolness, Steve went hunting for concessions. I noticed Scott squinting in the sun, making shade with his palm and fingers over a perspiring brow. The realization hit. Scott was the only boy not wearing a hat. He had asked me once last week and I had forgotten until my son stood in the hot sun without relief. Mother of the year, indeed.

When he came off the field I said, "You're a natural! How about we get you a hat?" We picked up a treat and he revived like a plant after summer rain.

When Steve needed something he pestered me, but that wasn't Scott's style. What an easy pattern could develop, giving all my attention to the most assertive child or needy twins while neglecting a boy who would only ask once. I would do better. If Scott mustered the effort to ask, I would respond.

I think Jim realized that I needed a break, so he took me on a date. Nothing too expensive, just dinner since the twins were still small. As we drove, he spotted a "For Sale" sign on a piece of commercial land and he stopped so I could jot down the telephone number. That was one of his best methods for finding property and he had an eye for site selection, but I was annoyed and said so. "Can't we leave business for *two hours*?"

Not long after that, Jim wanted to go see some property up Ogden Canyon and we reminisced about a simpler time when we'd escape with a McDonald's burger and nothing but the river and each other. We reached a sign marking a new subdivision to be called Nordic Valley, adjacent to where a ski resort had recently opened.

It was a beautiful spot and he said, "Bill Wood is building a cabin up here. What if we did, too?" It was love at first sight, and he already had the numbers worked out. The developer required monthly payments of $50, quite a bit to us, but manageable.

We bushwhacked through a scrub oak landscape, with jays squawking, squirrels scurrying, and undergrowth in shadow. It was still green on that side of the mountain. Any sounds of humans that day were swallowed up in the vegetation and the rhythm of breath while our sneakers snapped twigs underfoot. In sunny spots, the hillside smelled of cheat grass baked blonde and dusty sagebrush, the scent seeping into our clothes and hair. The shade smelled green, almost spicy. We talked about enjoying weekends up there: skiing, hiking, cool summer evenings, and clear skies in winter. I had two requirements, though.

"No television and no dishwasher."

I wanted us to spend time together, for the kids to learn to do dishes and talk while cleaning up each evening. I might even laugh if they told an inappropriate joke here and there.

Jim began taking a crew up on weekends to work on it. He did what he could himself and had good help with the rest. He went on the alert for salvaged fixtures and turned up with some damaged cabinets for free from a vendor. When finished, the cabin came to 700 square feet with two bedrooms and an orange acorn fireplace in the middle. We splurged on cedar paneling for the inside, which made it rustic and cozy. Our first overnighter was the Fourth of July weekend in 1971.

From the time the cabin was finished, we loaded the station wagon nearly every Friday evening year-round and headed out about five o'clock, winter and summer. We wouldn't return until Sunday evening. It became tradition to stop at the 7-Eleven on Washington Boulevard to buy comic books, one candy item each, and some soda pop on the way up.

During the winter, we skied right off our property to Nordic Valley and traversed back at dusk. In the summer time, the boys hiked or rode bikes. We played games like Crazy Eights and Pictionary. As the kids became better skiers, we frequented Powder Mountain, favoring Nordic for night skiing. We later bought a water skiing boat and all the kids became very good. The boys did stunts and the twins were so agile they could get up with a pinky and Bonnie skied on one ski.

Steve had made a ping pong table in shop class and we put it on bricks to serve as our dining table. We sat Japanese style, adjacent to the galley kitchen and fireplace. When the weather was nice, we put a little table for the twins to eat outside. I smiled at how easy cleanup was with a hose whenever they spilled juice. After dinner and game time each night, the boys would decide where to put their sleeping bags and the three girls slept in bunk beds.

As years went on and we replaced furniture at home, the older models went up to the cabin including the chrome and red Formica table we had shipped from Canada after we first moved to Ogden. In this way, the cabin became a repository for memories of earlier years, even as we made new memories together there.

Bill Wood and family often visited our cabin for dinner and we regularly stopped by theirs. We thought it was amusing when Bill once showed us a photograph of himself taken from behind while cross country skiing, buck naked.

One Friday evening we rolled into the 7-Eleven with the station wagon's rear sagging. I packed the vacuum, toaster, and other appliances we needed because we only owned one of everything. Our poodle was also in there somewhere. Jim gassed up and the rest of us trotted inside.

Bonnie picked out her candy and asked me, "Can I have this, too?"

I said, "Go ask your dad," and she tilted her head as if debating how bad she wanted it. She put it back on the shelf. We checked out and piled in, the boys disappearing onto rear-facing seats behind our appliances.

Some way up the road, Jim was chatting away and he asked, "Steve, what do you think?" No reply. "Steve? Steve?"

Scott announced, "He's not here, Dad."

I whipped around and Jim growled, "He's what?"

I could hear Scott grinning, "We left Steve at the store." When we pulled back into the parking lot, he was sitting on the curb of the bowling alley next door trying to look cool.

Once I remember forgetting diapers and Jim had to make a late-night run to the store. In the morning, I found a single rose he had picked up for me, too. That's one thing about Jim Kier. He was a man's man, and sometimes even gruff, but he nearly always brought me back a little something from the store: a piece of candy, a magazine, or flowers. There is more than one way to say, "I love you."

My only guilt was that we missed church during those years. Jim worked such grueling hours that he needed to rest, and I didn't have the heart to wake everybody for church. I hoped God would forgive me but I could not shortchange our family time. In retrospect, that cabin became a form of salvation—I believe it saved our family.

In 1972 we were looking for an affordable family vacation and learned you could rent a houseboat on Shuswap Lake in British Columbia. We needed no extra entertainment and could cook our own meals. All the children would enjoy it, although I made the twins keep lifejackets on the entire time except to sleep.

We had a wonderful time and took turns diving off the top into glacier-fed water. After the children were all asleep, I skinny dipped off the back of the boat while Jim had a drink and urged me to hurry.

"Get in here! Somebody will see you. What if the kids wake up?"

I just hollered back up, "It's too dark for anybody to see," and enjoyed myself. I never could get Jim to join me.

GROWING

◼

We got involved in the Weber Basin Homebuilder's Association and in 1973, they announced the upcoming national convention in Houston. Salt Lake and Ogden home builders were abuzz with plans to catch a Caribbean cruise out of Houston afterward.

Jim studied our budget and said, "We should go to the national convention. It's important to keep up on the latest." We called a travel agent and decided to join the cruise, too. The idea of getting away without kids was, quite simply, a dream.

Jim said, "What is the point of working so hard if we never enjoy the freedom of our own business?"

I lost sleep the whole week before, worrying about something happening to the kids while we were gone. Before this trip, we had experienced precious little alone time because our parents were so far away. We took the kids everywhere with us. While I wrung my hands, the kids were excited to have their grandparents come. We hyped it up and then we were off, promising gifts and hugs upon return.

I told myself it would be fine, but had to redo my makeup several times the first day because every time someone asked who was looking after our children, the tears would come and I had to fix black streaks on my face.

We deplaned in Houston and once my separation anxiety wore off, the trip fed our minds and rested our spirits. Jim likened the conference registration fee to college tuition.

As we ate a quick bite in the conference center, Jim said, "I noticed some people cutting out early to get drinks. What an extravagant waste of time." In this spirit, we were waiting there when the door opened and stayed until the closing announcement.

As we walked the show together, Jim spotted the holy of holies. His step quickened in a beeline toward a double booth with shelves of industry books. These were titles you simply couldn't get through our public library or local booksellers. Watching him flush with a hungry gleam, I fell in love with my husband all over again. His eye did a quick scan, like a first pass through a buffet before putting anything on his plate. Then he began handling them one-by-one, giving each one its due respect. He walked as if on sacred ground and I understood that he did believe knowledge was sacred. Books were the physical artifacts. I could see his eyes aflame with a desire to consume every last word. He made some selections right away, but he'd consider others more carefully during the conference. After ten minutes or so, I left Jim to his personal worship. We could rendezvous later and I had whole walls of carpet and paneling and light fixture samples to inspect anyway.

He must have purchased thirty books that trip—which had to be shipped back—and he heaped them on the hotel room floor. He circled the hill as if he were a neighborhood kid with a dirt bike, waiting to play on a construction mound. I asked how much it would cost to get them home and he said, "If I get just one idea out of each book, it will be worth the price."

This trip began a lifelong kinship between Jim and the booksellers. At the next convention, they were like school chums. When we moved from our home across from Emerald Hills to our present house, the boys had to heft Jim's library up and down stairs. Reading is a virtue, but I doubt professional movers feel that way.

That first trip to the convention fed our minds for the next two years until we attended again. The convention and the books did help Jim become an expert. Although he was still young, people began seeking for his advice.

When the convention ended, we boarded the Romanza and let our cares melt into aqua blue seas. I had packed a long gold evening gown and some play clothes including a sunny yellow pantsuit with a long blouse with fringe, a fun little number for dancing because the fringe flounced with every shimmy. Each evening I did my hair into a bouffant style with some pieces pulled back and curled ends. As a bonus, it made me look taller. One evening they held a "Ms. Romanza" contest and Jim told the others how I had been in the Miss Eskimo pageant in Edmonton.

They nudged me to enter and I blushed, "I'm too shy."

My heart began pounding because they were all in fine form and not likely to let me off the hook. Finally—*very* reluctantly—I went up there. I was stunned to be selected as the first runner up, especially at nearly 40, and post-twins. We found the Caribbean an absolute paradise with all the wonderful calypso music and the warm water, quite an adventure for two Canadian birds.

On our flight home, Jim began experiencing stomach distress and had to get up for the bathroom several times. I wondered if he had eaten something bad, but in subsequent years this would be the same routine each time we traveled. On the flight back, Jim would begin worrying about the business again and after full relaxation, his body had an adjustment period.

The year before, we had incorporated and created Kier Corporation from what had been Kier Construction, a sole-proprietorship of Jim and Norma Kier. We were growing enough that the foot traffic in our home was becoming too much. We had plans to build the Glenmore Manor apartment complex in Washington Terrace, a series of four-plexes, and the city allowed us to move our offices into a single unit. Happy day! What a huge milestone for our company—and mostly for our family. After ten years of commerce through our doors, we could now have a private home life.

I got help with the twins earlier, and as business picked up, had stopped cleaning the homes myself, too. Now the decorating and secretarial duties were outpacing me and we needed more help in the office. Up until this point we had only hired superintendents and construction workers, but we finally accepted that it was time to hire a secretary.

When Jim and I went out of town again, we put Steve Bailey in charge of the office. Rich Hagen and Steve Bailey decided to wrap up this detail for us. Among the candidates was a bright young woman named Annette Peterson. One of our employees had been going into the Standard Examiner to place classifieds for our spec homes and was impressed with her in that department.

"You should come to work with us at Kier Corporation," he said. When the position opened, she applied, Steve Bailey and Rich held interviews and offered the job.

When we returned, Steve Bailey reported to Jim on all the work he'd accomplished including, "And I filled the assistant position."

Jim was taken aback, "Don't you think I should meet my own secretary?"

Steve called Annette back, "Would you come in to meet Jim Kier?"

She said that was a good idea, so she came into the office and I immediately liked her—we clicked right away.

Jim thanked her for coming in and said, "If we hire you, when would you like to start?"

She blinked and responded, "You already have, and I start on Monday." *That's the spirit*, I thought. Jim concurred with Steve's decision, and it turned out to be one of the important decisions of our lives. She was still with us 45 years later.

In just a year, the workload emanating from Jim's brain had outgrown even Annette's capable skills, so we advertised for help with bookkeeping, accounts payable, and general office work. We extended an offer to someone, but fate had a different plan. That girl was a no-show, so Jim called his second choice, a slender young woman named Margo Bench.

Steve and Scott were out on job sites all summer, and we hoped they would grow into bigger roles. That would present challenges that we hoped to mitigate by setting the stage in advance.

Jim said, "We will treat employees like family, and the kids will have to work twice as hard to earn the employees' respect."

Another key hire was the mild-mannered and clean-cut Burrell Davis as our Property Manager. All of us were crowded into that single apartment unit and Burrell's orientation included instructions on office etiquette.

"This is the bathroom. Right here is a desk." Jim stretched his arms, touching one hand on the bathroom door the other on an in-basket. Also on the desk was a can of air fresher. He nodded toward it, "This is the air spray. Kindly use it."

Another office assistant at the time drove a beautiful yellow Z-28, and she warned Burrell, "Don't park anywhere near Jim unless you want your bumper crunched or your door dinged. His head is in the work," and motioning toward her car said, "not out here with the rest of us."

She parked her car on the street where Jim couldn't get near. I knew how she felt. At home, we now had a three-car garage and I first parked in the middle next to Jim's car, but soon took over the outer spot, giving Jim wide berth. The garage doors had to be replaced six or seven times after he yanked the car into reverse without so much as a mirror glance.

One morning Jim came into the office wearing his daily uniform: tan pants, a sport coat, and ankle boots to give an extra inch of height. The boots were always the same with a zipper on the side but in blue, black, tan, or gray.

He walked to Annette's desk and she said, "Your boots are different colors." He looked down and noticed that one was tan and one was gray. He shrugged, she smiled, and he put a newspaper clipping on her desk.

"It says this man needs a wheelchair. Will you find out who he is and donate one?" She scanned the article and her eyes met his and he said, "Just don't tell anybody where it came from. Anonymous. Got that?"

She nodded, "Sure boss. What a kind thing to do," but he waved it off and ran to one of Steve's projects.

At the job site, someone spotted Jim's truck coming and hollered, "Jim Kier's pulling up!" Everyone straightened at their post and picked up debris within reach. He jumped out with notes in hand and Steve trotted over to follow him around. He wasn't like a puppy worshiping the boss, but more like a shepherd, steering him away from danger.

By this time, we had outgrown our office space and needed to take over Unit #2. Our Section 8 work with HUD was taking off and before long we moved into another and then finally occupied all four units. Now Kier Corporation operated sub-departments within the company: the development side of things, construction, interior design, and property management. During that time, Bill Wood called and Margo set about tracking Jim down. She paged to Unit #2, which replied that he was just there but was now in Unit #3. She called there but he had already gone to #4. By the time she got #4 on the line, he had driven off in his Buick.

Bill came by the office with a ponytail and Birkenstocks. He had recently transitioned from his 9-5 banker persona into a Willie Nelson type. He was done working for the man and everyone in the office had taken to calling him Wild Bill. He had some property, a little cash, and two partners with the last names Anderson and Dillard. They approached Bill about a Section 8 HUD project and after flipping through the figures, Jim said, "It'll fly."

Over the coming weeks, the HUD docs were drafted and Bill stopped by our office to review before submitting. They paged through the whole project one last time and Bill stepped into the restroom, came out, and Jim faked a choke.

"For the love of Pete, Bill, some air freshener please."

They went back and forth about whether a "pine scented crapper" (in Jim's Scottish accent) is better or worse than an unadulterated job, until Jim got back to business, "We're done, just one blank here. What are you calling this project?"

Bill looked sly and said, "How about FTG Square?"

Jim penciled it in while saying aloud "F-T-G," then put the stack in a folder.

On his way out, Bill had a spring in his step, "I like the sound of that. F-T-G. Has a ring."

Jim hollered while faking a gag, "Definitely pine, Bill! Anything but this stink."

One of the secretaries typed up the paperwork and handed him the stack, which Jim hefted out to his car for review. A few minutes later, he returned to the office.

"I need help. FTG papers are scattered from here to hell."

He rounded several of us up and we caravanned to trace his route and salvage whatever we could.

"Which way did you go home?" we asked.

Jim replied, "I don't remember."

Steve rolled his eyes, "Absent minded professor." We took the most likely street where papers clung to fences and plastered sidewalks. We recovered all we could, with some gone forever. Secretaries, attorneys, and title company folks buckled down to redo what was missing.

While Jim was developing his personal business rules during these years, our employees were writing their own version. First on the list had been "use air freshener," and the second they added was "never give Jim Kier an original."

Burrell came into the office from inspecting apartments, then he and Jim briefed each other. Jim handed him a fresh task list and added, "Oh, and we finally cleaned up the FTG fiasco and mailed it to HUD today."

Burrell got a funny look on his face, "What do you think of the name?"

Jim answered, "Not my concern. It's Bill's building."

Burrell asked, "But you're okay with it? "

Jim shrugged while scooping up papers, "It's Bill's name on the deed."

Burrell prodded, "Still, it's your relationship with HUD..." but Jim was already out the door. Burrell mulled over what to say when they talked again, but was interrupted by a blood-curdling scream. Burrell and Steve's hearts stopped and they raced outside. Was a child hit? The secretary stood by the curb frozen, her hands on her cheeks.

"What's wrong?"

She pointed to her Z-28 and a crumpled bumper, "Jim backed right into my car and drove away."

Margo mused, "Poor man. He has absolutely no idea."

The secretary looked at her car and looked at Margo with a dazed expression, "Poor *man*?"

Jim came in the next day and asked Annette, "Heard anything about FTG?" She pursed her lips and shook her head.

Burrell looked up and studied Jim's face and asked, "It's still FTG?"

Jim said, "It's growing on me. Has a ring to it."

Burrell said, "Have time for lunch?"

Jim caught an importance in the tone and stopped, "Sure."

They headed out and over a drink Jim said, "I'm still kicking myself over the FTG delay." Burrell shifted in his chair, searching for words.

Jim set down a glass and asked, "What's with you and that project? It'll be a winner."

Burrell said, "I've no doubt. It's just...you do know what that means, right?"

Jim looked blank, "The inner workings of Wild Bill's mind don't concern me. "

Burrell blinked, "Bill is having a field day with you." Jim looked puzzled.

Burrell gulped the last liquid courage and launched in, "Jim, my friend, when Army guys say F-T-G, it means F*&# the Government."

Jim dropped his fork.

"Could the people at HUD know?" Then thinking aloud to himself, "They're not known for a sense of humor."

With eyes flashing, Jim rushed Burrell out the door and they hauled back to the office, rushing back in like a tsunami.

"Book me to Denver, make an appointment at HUD, and get Bill's sorry ass on the line." He played with his ear and paced the twenty feet of our office until Bill picked up. Jim closed the door to have words, but everyone could hear through the walls anyway.

"You think you're funny? This is my *reputation*."

His voice never rose to quite a yell and a while later Bill slinked in with a giant bottle of Chivas. They had a drink and Jim stomped out to make a point, but when I looked close, I saw an ever-so-slight twinkle in his eye. Bill had got him good.

Jim got off the elevator at the HUD office, wearing humility like a uniform.

"I am so sorry. Honestly, I had no idea. Zero."

They believed him. They liked him. And that's why they made the change with correction fluid rather than being difficult just to prove a point. They could have made us resubmit and then relegated it to the bottom of the pile.

Upon return, he took Steve and Scott aside to tell them, "Remember this. You treat your customers, your subs, and even government partners like gold and they'll come through when you need them."

During those years, Annette learned everything about property management and we came to rely on her attention to detail and her loyalty for keeping us out of trouble. Whenever a question came up, Jim became famous for saying, "Ask Annette." He learned the hard way what happened when he did not.

In 1974 I turned 44 and although this wasn't a milestone birthday, we were in a contemplative mood at dinner. It was a Sunday night and we thought about the coming workweek. Maybe it was the fact that Jim had just turned 48, inching toward the big five-oh that led him to say, "In the thirteen years since we started Kier Construction, we've worked non-stop. The point of having your own business is to get what you want out of life."

I added, "We are very, very blessed, and there is so much I still want to do."

He tousled his hair as if to tease out an idea, then said, "I've been reading about the power of writing goals down. Let's make a list of everything we still want to do."

We realized that our lives had focused entirely around the kids and the business up to that point and nothing we wanted to do for ourselves. For the rest of the evening, we daydreamed together of plans we still had, and before bed we took it to a pen and pad. My list included learning to play tennis, Paris, and someday owning a little piece of Canada. At the top of Jim's list was visiting his ancestral home in Scotland, getting a sailboat, and going back to see The Gang in Ottawa. We both wanted to travel more, anywhere and everywhere we could.

It took nearly a year for me to find a tennis instructor and I was afraid to look foolish because I'd never had a racket in my hand. Was I already too old to learn a new sport? Can I still run? Of course I had been running after children, but I had not been on a formal exercise routine in ages. I learned there was a new tennis club being built, so five ladies signed up for eight lessons that would be held at noon on Fridays. I felt out of shape at first, but learned that my eyesight and aim were good. Maybe that was from being in the Rifle Club back in Wainwright. I loved this sport even more than I expected and have played at least twice a week since then.

That year for Christmas we decided to take the family on our biggest trip ever: Hawaii. We began making plans and it worked well because Jenny and Bob wanted to use the cabin while we were gone. We ran into a snag, though. The boys were on the Bonneville High wrestling team and could not go. They had practices and matches through the holidays and they were on strict diets, too. I also suspected they were in cahoots.

If they played their cards right, we might leave them home alone. Not a chance.

Steve and Jim were already butting heads over the mess in his room and his attitude, "Steve, you are the eldest and an example to the others. This is not acceptable."

Steve would stomp off and refuse to clean his room on Saturday when we required the other kids to do theirs. Jim responded by throwing Steve and Scott's clothes on the snow-covered lawn while the girls stood open-mouthed. Scott managed to stay on good terms with all parties.

So leaving them home for the holidays wasn't happening and we canceled Hawaii to all stay in the cabin with Jenny and Bob. By the way, Bob sold industrial flooring for a British company and his territory included Utah. This enabled them to visit us regularly as he was covering his region.

During the holidays, the girls and I stayed up until 1 a.m. making Mum's cookie recipes and walnut rolls, an annual tradition. On Christmas Eve I cooked a turkey, my mum's wonderful stuffing and pumpkin pie recipes, and the boys came out of their rooms howling at the smell, famished by wrestling-deprivation. We stayed up late laughing and playing games and on Christmas morning, everyone else padded out to the tree. I was still in the bathroom, "Wait a minute, I have to put my face on." The family groaned, but I wanted to be presentable for the pictures.

When the break was over, we went to a wrestling match and it pleased me to see my strong, rebellious teenage boys walk onto the floor and look for their parents. I would never miss a match.

On this particular evening there were three unfortunate events. The first was when, in a frenzy of excitement, I jumped up and my heel came down on Jim's foot. The second was more serious. Steve's opponent made a move and I could see from the stands how his elbow was skiwampus. He let out a yelp and before the ref could pull the other kid off, I jumped across people and ran down onto the mat. I didn't realize until afterward that my heels had poked holes into the mat. Steve said those holes were there for years and his friends teased him, "From your mommy's heels." By now the other boy's father was also down on the mat arguing with the ref. I stood my tallest and exchanged words about his behavior. The next time we attended a meet, Jim sat away from me, for his safety and emotional comfort. I never knew how Jim could be so calm in a game or match for one of our kids.

In early summer before Steve's senior year, Jim had asked Steve to report to work, but before Steve headed out, Jim called him in to listen on a call.

It was the superintendent yelling, "I don't want no F**ing boss's kid on my job site. They're cocky but still need their asses wiped."

Jim defended our son, "He's a damn hard worker. "

They hung up and Steve asked, "So where do you want me to go?"

Jim was unfazed, "Where I told you."

When Steve showed up, the superintendent growled, "Why in hell are you here?"

Steve stood his ground. "I was told to report to work here."

The superintendent assigned him an entire slab to grade by himself, probably thinking it was like loading a truck with bricks—that it would keep Steve out of everybody's hair. When he finished it, he was given another, and then another. Steve did not complain, stubbornness pushing him to prove a point. By the middle of summer, the superintendent had promoted Steve to be his assistant.

After putting away some savings, Steve came to Jim with a request to co-sign on a loan for a Jeep. Jim gave in, but only after a stern lecture about the consequence for missing a payment or reckless driving. Steve took it on the chin but rolled his eyes a little.

We urged Steve to start college. At the time, hardly anyone in the construction industry had a degree, but Jim wanted his sons to shine.

"I dreamed of going to college," Jim told him. "You have that chance, so don't squander it," but Steve kept postponing his application to Weber State.

Right before the application deadline, one evening Steve did not come home and left a note on the kitchen counter. It said that he was grateful for the opportunity to go to college, and he was sorry to disappoint us, but "I'm not the college type." He said he loved construction and that he was learning more on the job than he would in any class. He wanted to work with his hands. Steve's decision was final.

Buried under Jim's frustration was also a pride in his son that he couldn't quite let show. Our son, raised on the job site, now just wanted to be in construction with us.

Steve turned 18 and had his head so full of girls and rebellion that father and son locked horns just about any time they were in a room together. It was bad. The ongoing conflict made home life stressful for the whole family, and when I say Steve was rebellious, I am softening the reality a great deal. Our patience had worn through and more to the point, we were worried that Steve was headed for more serious trouble if he did not straighten up his act. We decided to put our son on notice before we left on a trip to Hawaii (just the two of us).

Jim gave Steve a list written on a pre-printed pad with the standardized project header where Jim filled in:

"Project: Steve Kier. Date: Feb-16/76"

1. Repair fence. Pick up material at Wheelwright
2. Count # of grape stakes needed to repair
3. Maintain & keep garage clean. Floor & shelves.
4. Time limit on telephone 3 min.
5. Assist Scott with garage Wed night
6. Run all errands for around house, ex: food store, dry cleaning, drug store etc. Kids on special functions.
7. Supper clean up Wed. nite. Includes mopping floor.
8. Clean outside windows when needed.
9. Always keep room & bathroom in order. Any clothes not hung up will be thrown out. Clean glass on shower door.
10. Keep up on own clothes. Learn ironing & washing.
11. Responsible to keep all cars clean on inside weekly. Pick own nite during week.
12. Don't take this lightly! If in doubt, talk to Dad.
13. Summer assist in general yard maintenance, yard work, up keep of house.
14. Hair cut once a month. All school nites in at 10 pm

On the back Jim wrote:

1. If these duties are not acceptable then I suggest you make arrangements to pay $50 room & board to justify the work that other people are doing for you.
2. Lack of cooperation results in Jeep grounded for 3 nites.
3. Second offense 1 week and so on.

Then we flew into paradise and gave ourselves a break. From the first moment, I fell in love with Hawaii as my new happy place. We returned many times over the years, once even meeting up with my brother Jon. I had really missed him, and after dinner I kicked my shoes off and danced with him like old times. We thought we were dancing well until a group of professional dancers entered the scene and we conceded the floor.

We got back and found that the twins had acted up a bit by spreading Vaseline all over their green-checkered bedspreads, saying they did it because they missed us, but Steve did a pretty good job. It did not take long after we were back, though, for Steve to commit multiple infractions related to The List. Jim got mad, Steve back-talked, and Jim stormed in loaded for bear.

"This house isn't big enough for both of us. You've got five minutes to get out," and Jim helped the process by starting to throw Steve's things out onto a snow-covered lawn while the twins stood watching. Steve took the punch list with him, proof of his father's unreasonableness.

When he showed a buddy, his friend asked, "Can I have that?"

Steve tossed it, "Gladly."

We did not hear directly from Steve for six months. I was heartsick. We had no idea of his whereabouts, although after a while we learned through Scott that he was safe and rooming with a friend. A while later he began calling me, and I acted as intermediary if Steve and Jim needed to convey information to each other. I did my best to back Jim up while expressing unconditional love and a desire for the two of them to work it out. I worried so much about how he was and came to think of this era as the heartbreak years.

Steve eventually told me where he was living—some sort of college-age commune apartment—so Bonnie and I brought him a care package. During this time, he never missed reaching out to me on holidays, sending cards or flowers.

Steve ended up working as a framer with Larry Olesky who had been employed by Jim and recently gone out to do his own carpentry finish work. Larry taught him so much and Steve was open when it was someone other than his dad.

After six months, Jim felt it was time to make amends, so one night when Steve left a friend's house, Jim was waiting on the curb with a six pack. They talked it out, although it took a full two years before Steve would consider coming back to work for Kier Construction.

Steve explained it this way, "I hate everybody thinking I'm just the boss's kid. I want to make it on my own. "

Jim respected that, but kept after him, "You will prove yourself, and you already have solid experience. Steve, you have the makings of a leader and the truth is, we could really use your talent. Sky's the limit for you."

This rare openness worked and Steve did eventually return, took a pay cut, and moved back home to offset it. After six or seven more months, Steve understood that the house was indeed too small for both of their personalities, so he moved out again.

After he left, Jim muttered to me, "I don't know where he *gets* it. " And he was serious. I don't think he ever did see it.

1976 - 1982

INDEPENDENCE

———◆———

In 1976, we received an invitation from General Electric to attend an annual trip they hosted for their best appliance customers. We had built up to this status by purchasing GE appliances exclusively for our homes and apartments and had done a brisk business the past year. GE always arranged for a luxury trip at a highly-subsidized price, this time to Italy. We had never been somewhere so exotic and had many opportunities to dress up and see sites we had only seen in books. My parents came to stay with the kids.

The next GE trip was in 1977 to Hong Kong and we went every year for a while, then every two years. Those trips were spectacular. In Hong Kong they had booked a premiere hotel right on the water and we sat transfixed on our balcony watching a whole city about its routine in the harbor below. Big families lived on little boats and a grocery boat zoomed around making deliveries. We lost track of time and ended up being late for dinner in an evening gown and tuxedo. They had rolled out an actual red carpet to the ballroom door. The food was unparalleled the entire trip and the GE planners kept us busy with tours and activities, including an outing to the garment district where they had scheduled for each of us to meet with a tailor. We selected fabric and had a custom suit made. I liked mine and wore it a lot, but Jim was not a big fan of suits in the first place and there was something a little too flashy about his. It turned out to be a fun but impractical souvenir for my husband until we finally donated it. We slept the full flight home so tired from not wanting to miss anything and also shopping for everyone. After that year, we never missed the opportunity to go on a GE trip, which meant we alternated every other year to attend the homebuilder's association trip and then with a GE tour: Greece, Switzerland, Japan, the Canary Islands, and more.

One moment that stands out from a trip in Germany was when we stayed in a really nice hotel where they put chocolate on the pillows each evening. We awoke after a romantic evening and took one look at each other before cracking up; we had melted chocolate smeared on our faces and hair. We hadn't noticed the unwrapped treats, making us look like we'd had a really good time. We were mortified at the hotel staff having to clean the linens, though.

From that point on, we added new employees at a steady pace. By 1979 we had outgrown Glenmore Manor in Washington Terrace and Jim went in search of a permanent facility with room to grow. The Gorder Station Post Office on Quincy Avenue was coming available so Jim and I went to look at it. The location was central, the price was right, and it was a well-constructed shell that we could configure. We acted on the property, but any government transaction takes a while. We also had to build our offices on the inside. They turned out attractive and adequate, suiting us well. We moved from the Glenmore Manor apartments into the new building on Quincy on November 27, 1981.

After starting to work in the business again, Jim went into professor mode with Steve and Scott. Both boys had worked up from general laborers to framers and Scott was becoming a fine craftsman. He took a great deal of pride in his work, and his attention to detail was noticed by anyone with an eye for it. He thrived on this work and aspired to become a master craftsman, already having built his first home and amassed his own shop of tools. He led us through his home and talked about the details. Scott wasn't one to turn attention on himself, but he would let a spotlight shine on the work.

Steve earned his place as a Superintendent before he was 21. Not just on little jobs, either. He was overseeing entire subdivisions with maybe 50 low-income single-family homes. In that role, Jim would leave him to it with high expectations and little oversight. Jim just made sporadic appearances and whenever Steve got wind that his dad was planning a visit, he would crack the whip and work like mad on weekends to spit-shine the whole project. The entire jobsite sparkled before Jim Kier showed up.

After Scott graduated from high school, Jim pulled him aside, "You have a natural attention to detail. We need an estimator, and you would make a great one."

Scott was shy about it, "Me? I want to work with my hands. And I took a test that said stay away from numbers."

Jim brushed that aside, "Tests mean nothing. You have the perfect mix of field experience and the right disposition." He set Scott up in an office, "Let's see how it goes."

Scott would enjoy craftsmanship as an outlet for the rest of his life, but from day one he was an exceptional estimator. At first he asked a lot of advice, but as time wore on, he became the resident expert.

Scott enrolled for a semester at Weber State, and you know what his favorite class was? The one where he learned a skill to use for the rest of his life: tallying numbers with a ten-key. By the time his grades came out, his fingers went tappity-tap without his eyes ever looking at the yards of adding machine tape curling out the back.

Jim found an excellent construction management program in Denver and flew out with Scott to meet the Dean. They were impressed and Jim was hopeful, but Scott kept putting his application off.

Jim pushed the issue until Scott finally broke it to him, "Ogden is my home. I love the business, I love being an estimator, and I don't want to leave." Scott came closer to asking for understanding, "Dad, I want you to be proud of me, but I'm not learning anything in college. I'm meant for construction, not the classroom." Later, the boys would say that they went to the "Jim Kier School of Hard Knocks," even as they looked to hire people with a university degree.

Scott had a wonderful outside mentor in those years, Jack Cox, from Wheelwright Lumber. He trained Scott like a son. This was another example of how each one of our kids had someone take them under their wing and train them in a way that a parent can never get away with. Scott took his on-the-job training as seriously as Steve had, although Scott would seek out his dad's advice from time to time.

"This bid looks too low. What should I do?"

Jim taught the important lesson, "Treat your employees and subs like you would family. Tell them it looks off and give a chance to resubmit."

Scott called, but the owner was adamant, "I've checked it, it looks good."

But Scott knew it wasn't and pulled the bid.

After it closed, the owner called in a panic, "I found it." Scott told him that he had not used the figure. The sub lost the job, but both parties had been relieved of an unworkable burden.

"You're a pal. Your dad would've done the same thing. I'll listen to you next time."

The boys honed their instincts. Steve had his dad's ability to pick winners and pass on stinkers. Scott developed an uncanny sense for sniffing out errors. Even on complex projects with hundreds of moving parts, he could look at a number and tell it was off. His time swinging a hammer and pouring concrete gave him an innate sense of how long a job should take. Whatever standardized test he had taken was dead wrong about his aptitude for finessing numbers. There's more to that skill than "if train X leaves at Y speed." Scott also balanced duty to the developer's bottom line, loyalty to our family of subs, and commitment to our own company's profitability. They made mistakes, but as a team, their batting average was good.

We still went to the cabin most weekends and had remodeled it to add on space. Now it was quite comfortable when we had guests. Everyone had a bed and we put a dining room off the kitchen. Even though Steve was on his own now, Jim would call and say, "Your mom and I want to go boating," and Steve would come, drive us to the dam, back the boat into the water, and usually leave until he retrieved us at dusk. Jim loved taking the boat out, but shied away from getting it to the water: hitching, safety, remembering it was attached while driving, and backing it into the drink. He almost sunk the boat a couple times after forgetting to put the plug in.

One bluebird Sunday we were meeting our friend Jim Stacy on Willard Bay and Steve couldn't take us, so Jim did the routine himself and hollered for me and the girls to hop in. We piled into the truck in

swimsuits under shorts and all of us were talking as we rounded the corner. A block below our house on Woodland Drive, we hit a bump and
Jim tapped the brakes. I startled as something caught my attention outside the window. I gasped.

"The boat is passing us!" I yelled.

It gained momentum before obliterating a hand-carved mailbox
with seagulls and nautical ornamentation as the boat found its angle of
repose on what had been a perfectly manicured lawn.

Jim got out of the truck sputtering and the homeowner ran toward
us hot under the collar. Jim couldn't apologize enough.

"I will replace your mailbox."

But the neighbor had to vent, *"Replace?* It was one of a kind! How
could this have even happened?"

Jim shook his head, but the post was not cranked up, the latch not
down, and the safety chain not connected. At first bump, the hitch
bounced off the ball and that was the extent of our fun for the day.
Neighbors gathered around and I heard one say, "I can't wait to see what
the Kiers will do next."

In 1981, Jim booked an Alaskan fishing trip for him, the two boys,
Burrell, and some other employees. I took the girls to Nassau in the Ba-
hamas. The boys flew into Vancouver where they spent the first night
staying up late and telling stories. Early the next morning, the group
boarded a seaplane into Ketchikan, Alaska, where they charted a boat
for primitive camping and glorious fishing upriver. The first afternoon
while fishing the deep river, Jim told Scottish jokes he had been saving
for the trip. That evening they got a safety lesson.

"Make noise. Lots of noise. Bears will scamper off if they hear you
coming, but if you startle a mama bear, it's game over."

With long Alaskan summer days, it felt natural to stay up until midnight talking freely under the protective shroud of a boys' secrecy pact,
although these things have a way of coming out eventually.

Late night aside, they emerged at 4 a.m. into a chilly Alaskan morning. By mid-day they disembarked to clomp up a melting icicle of a trib-
utary. The scenery was astounding: even when overcast, the clearness of
the air disintegrated thoughts of work and opened a man up. Jim let go
and dropped his guard. Overcast skies deepened the forest greens and

they tracked salmon struggling upriver to spawn. Jim led rounds of Frere Jacques to alert bears. In subsequent trips, they watched from a distance where bears stood to swat great salmon out of the water, stunning them silly before flipping them ashore, then clambering onto the banks, ripping open their guts, and foundering on fish roe. It was such a lavish buffet that the bears would toss meat aside in favor of the next delicacy. Bald eagles and osprey circled high above then swooped down to polish off any remains, sometimes even swiping fish off hooks.

The two exuberant brothers hiked ahead toward a lake where the guide had directed, as Jim hollered, "Make noise!" Jim and Burrell stood on the bank to cast and reel their lures back in, cast and reel, cast and reel. They also breathed. Jim settled into a trancelike state and cast out, when the huge three-pronged hook caught on a branch behind him. His pole bent backward and he flicked the tip back and forth to set it free.

"Oh shit!"

Burrell whipped around, "What?"

Jim repeated, "Oh shit!" and then barked, "Burrell, get this damn hook off my head."

It had dislodged from the branches only to fling itself into the back of Jim's head. Burrell clomped over and directed Jim to reel in the excess of wispy line. He did, but perhaps a little too far, bowing his pole over his head with a brass and orange lure dangling above his thick mop.

"Get it out!"

Burrell examined the hook buried deep in Jim's hair and said, "I think we need the Captain's tools."

Jim grimaced, "Oh hell. So much for secrecy."

They gingerly made their way along the dry bank, Jim flattening his gait to minimize jostling that would make him wince. Now on deck, Jim was seated with the teardrop lure twisting like a leaf overhead.

The captain approached and Jim joked, "I caught something cap'n!"

He opened and closed his mouth in an O, making a fish sound. The captain approached, half amused and half frowning.

Jim repeated, "Get this damn thing out," adding, "would you please."

The captain had pliers, but after parting Jim's coal-colored hair, he pronounced a verdict.

"I've teased out many a hook, but I'm not touching that."

Jim looked disbelieving, "What the hell does that mean?"

The captain explained, "It means we're calling a plane that will deliver your sorry ass to a clinic in Ketchikan. That hook's in the bone." Hooks for catching king salmon are long and slick, and they're meant to burrow in deep.

Jim was glum, "Burrell, you'd better go get the boys." Burrell took off at an uneven run on the bank toward Steve and Scott who were oblivious.

He approached gasping and tried to shout above rushing water that sounded like a freeway. Once he was within earshot of the boys who stood in hip waders, Burrell hollered.

"Steve! Scott!"

They whipped around. With big arm motions Burrell waved them downstream. Out of breath from running, he called out, "Your dad's hurt."

They took off toward him lugging gear and slipping on mossy rocks. Adrenaline amped their bodies up, fearing a heart attack or a bear mauling. When they got close enough, Burrell calmed their fears.

"He's okay. He's fine, but he caught a hook in the back of his head. It's in deep so the captain is calling in a plane." The boys blinked, exhaled relief, and then became amused.

By the time they reached the boat, afternoon skies were clear and the Ketchikan Search and Rescue's seaplane had already lifted Jim away. When they asked the Captain if Jim was okay, he replied, "He had a stiff belt of Scotch on the plane and was fine after that." That night, the rest of the guys greedily rubbed their hands together at a windfall of material for ribbing Jim—this would carry them for years.

"He's the head of the family. The head of Kier companies. And now, the Alaskan Head Hooker."

The next morning, they fished the deep waters under the boat and listened for the plane to buzz in. Jim boarded wearing a new hat. He was grinning and lifted a hook with its blood-caked tip like a trophy. He then removed his hat and revealed a shaved patch of corpse-white skin on the back of his head. Before this, his scalp had been forever shielded from sunlight under an impenetrable forest of hair. In unison, the three gathered their poles and held them like spears, bowing, "Oh great one. We honor the fearsome Alaskan Head Hooker." A jovial mood carried the rest of the day.

By day four, the rocking boat and rhythm without a clock settled through them. Jim had already spent the jokes and funny stories he had collected beforehand. Fishing alongside each other, there was no longer a feeling that anyone needed to talk. Jim and Steve were standing together, with the others a little way off and Jim spoke in a tone that signaled importance. It was as if now, with banter finished, he could segue into a deeper purpose.

"Steve, we butt heads a lot and I sometimes wonder what in the hell you're *thinking*. I'm tough on you. But it's because I see natural leadership. You're smart, and a damn hard worker. You will be ready for more responsibility soon. You'll have to earn everyone's respect—no way around that—but if you do, there isn't anything you won't be capable of."

Steve listened. In other settings he might have taken issue with this part or that, but today he just took it in. There was an openness in the way Jim spoke, and such total focus, that Steve just absorbed the moment.

"You're already a superintendent. Someday you and Scott may lead the construction business and there are a few things I hope you will carry on. First, treat your customers like gold. Next, treat your employees like family and they will always be there for you. Be interested in their lives. Help them when they're in trouble and their loyalty will come through." He ran through mental notes before continuing.

"Third. Manage your risk and you will weather any market conditions. You've got to take risks to make money, but never more than you can afford if it goes south. Last, feed the company first. Always pay yourself after everything else. Lean up and put resources into the company, *especially* when there's not enough to go around. If you taste a little success and first thing you go buy a fancy truck and big house, those possessions will own you." He could have filled in stories to drive each point home, but he decided to leave the message clean. Simple doesn't mean easy, and he wanted these points to shine with clarity. If the boys learned only those four principles, they'd be alright.

Jim found a separate time to deliver the message to Scott. He led with Scott's unique strengths.

"People like being around you, Scott. Your laugh makes everyone happy. You've got an exceptional mind, and your even temperament is the perfect balance to Steve's hotheadedness. Someday, you and Steve will take turns in leadership." Scott always sought to back up his brother and still maintain a relationship with his dad.

In another mood, the boys might have resisted anything that hinted on a lecture. That day, though, on open water, Jim had the boys' full attention. Perhaps it was because they fully had Jim's.

Jim kept the tradition going every year after that.

Before trudging back to the office, Jim made them all reaffirm the pact to keep silent and he really didn't want me told about the hook. I wonder how long he thought he could wear a hat?

While they were fishing, we girls started our own tradition of lounging on the beach, going shopping and, as the girls got older, dancing. When the girls were adults, I remember that one afternoon we stopped in a club at happy hour for a few minutes, and ended up closing the place down.

The next night I suggested staying in, but we heard music coming from the resort's club and Kara said, "Oh Mum, you have the rest of your life to act old."

So I went, and as we entered, a whole group of sailors tumbled into the club. A handsome Naval Officer at least twenty years younger asked me to dance. Bonnie said, "Our Mum is *so shy*." The girls giggled and got a kick out of that.

When we all came back home refreshed and reluctant, I asked Jim how the trip was.

He was evasive, "Fine. Had a great time." When I spotted the boys they kind of ducked away, avoiding me and acting cagey. I wondered what they weren't telling me and was trying not to feel hurt.

In the meantime, one of them swiped the hook off Jim's desk and rushed it to a trophy shop. The boys got in touch with a bar we used to frequent on 36th Street and dropped off salmon for their staff to cook up. Fourteen of us got together for dinner and before the meal was served, Steve took a fork to a wine glass, "ting, ting, ting," to get everyone's attention. Steve, Scott, and Burrell stood in unison and called Jim to the front.

Steve—who was already becoming our family spokesman—took the lead: "When a man gets the catch of a lifetime, he hangs it on the wall. I doubt Dad will ever catch anything bigger, but we could not exactly mount Jim Kier's head. So we did the next best thing. We hereby present the infamous hook, with a little dab of Dad's blood right here."

Then he read the plaque, "Know all persons by these presents that James E. Kier will hereafter be known as 'Head Hooker of Alaska.'" Jim laughed with his whole body and was totally mortified. That plaque hung in our offices for many, many years.

Jim continued the annual trips with the boys, while the girls and I always picked a tropical spot. The next year, when the girls and I went to Hawaii, I got a frantic phone call that my dad had a heart attack. I got on the earliest flight I could with white knuckles the entire time, wondering if I would make it in time to see him. I got there in time to see him and he seemed fine. He had another heart attack a few days after I returned home and passed away at not quite 68 years old. I always remained close to both my Mum and Dad, ever a daddy's girl and often the one he would call or come down to see when he needed a listening ear in those later years. I loved him dearly, and the loss took something out of me for a while. I still get emotional sometimes when I think of my parents and all they went through and everything they sacrificed for me. Life doesn't stop for long, though, so I had to come home after staying with Mum for about a week following the funeral.

Not long after that, an official with HUD suggested that we set up my interior design work as a separate business and that I work as a subcontractor. For 20 years of business, I had never taken a paycheck, but the advice made legal sense and we wanted to stay in HUD's good graces.

Now in our new space, we put offices on one side and left the other half open as a warehouse for rolls of carpet in queue for large projects. I got my own office to meet with clients and launched Interiors by Norma. You know what? I thrived with my own company. I had the benefits of working with family, but when I handed out my crisp business cards, I got the same feeling as when I put on a new dress and heels. I felt a little taller. Jim had always deferred to my decorating decisions, but now it felt empowering to be entirely responsible for my own little piece of the Kier companies. Profitability was up to me and it felt good to meet with clients as a businesswoman in my own right.

I came home with a new pair of shoes one day, courtesy of a paycheck and sense of satisfaction. Jim tipped the box on its end to read the price and raised his eyebrows. I said something about how it had felt like a reward with *my* paycheck.

He replied, "You're doing pretty well. Good for you. Will you be leaving the Kier companies now?" On another day, I might have snipped back, but a wifely sense told me this wasn't jealousy, but wounded pride. Jim came from the old school and providing was a serious responsibility.

I applied salve, "Sweetheart, of course I'm not leaving. I love working with you and the kids. I wouldn't dream of doing anything else." He was reassured, and this became the new normal without further ado.

Without all my earlier duties, I was just as busy as ever, but this type of work played to my strengths. Oh sure there's a certain physical satisfaction to cleaning and a job well done, but scrubbing and typing payroll checks can get old.

Now Jim hired on another secretary to handle even more of his work life. No sooner had his new personal secretary become fully trained than she needed maternity leave. I suggested that another employee, Marie Hansen, take her place. Marie was sharp, energetic, and a very polite young lady we hired shortly after moving into the new office. In her interview, she had explained her background.

"I started at Weber, but intend to make a career of secretarial work. I have excelled at Thiokol, but the commute is a bear." She immediately took on all our Davis Bacon filings with the Feds to account for fair labor practices and had a knack for numbers. She could rattle them off the top of her head and seemed to thrive on both complexity and exactness. The only problem was that she too was pregnant and we wondered if she would come back after the baby.

Still, Jim asked if she would fill in for his secretary and she wanted to think about it. It was because Marie asked the current secretary, admitting, "I'm a little scared of him."

The current secretary said, "He is a very demanding boss, but you can handle the work...if you can handle *him*." The next day Marie agreed to fill in.

Marie and Jim clicked and she seemed to anticipate what he would need from the get-go. As his current secretary's leave ended, Jim asked Marie, "Would you consider staying in this position?" 1982 began a 23-year relationship with Marie as Jim's personal secretary that entire time, managing absolutely everything he needed done.

Shortly after Marie was hired, Jim clipped into the office and tossed off a hardhat without fixing his hair. He handed her some phone numbers scrawled on envelopes and asked, "Busy now?"

Marie's eyes had a she-tiger look as she compared an adding machine tape to a paper ledger. She held up a finger to signal "wait" and then her red pen pounced, "Gotcha!" She turned her chair toward him. "Not busy if you need me."

He said, "Big news. I need you to take notes at lunch." She retrieved her shorthand notebook—that blond was lightning fast.

They went inside the Horse where Dee Livingood from Big D construction motioned. Marie smoothed a pleated skirt and tucked in her blouse, sitting straight and ready to take notes.

"Relax, we'll get to business in time." Jim ordered a "Shirley Temple" for Marie, grinning. "There's no alcohol."

Marie looked around with interest, her eyes resting on an older man alone at the L-shaped bar nursing a drink and strumming his fingers.

Jim commented, "One of these times I'll see if the lacquer is worn through from his fingers if he's not sitting there. But he is always there. And that is why I plan to never retire."

Marie smiled and said, "This place reminds me of that new TV show, Cheers."

Jim and Dee nodded, "And hey, Marie looks a little like Diane."

Jim motioned toward her, "Except this girl isn't flighty." They bantered and got to business over sandwiches.

Dee said, "You've no doubt heard that President Reagan is visiting Hooper in September. The Party is asking for support from local businessmen. Here is a list of the logistics needed. Nobody wants to sponsor the port-a-potties. It's a critical detail with that many people in one place."

Jim said, "Put Kier down for that. We don't need recognition anyway."

They emerged into full-daylight shielding their eyes from the sun. Upon returning to the office, Jim pulled out a book where he kept records of donations and personal loans he made. He handed it over so Marie could begin keeping it for him.

That was early in our political involvement and it felt fun being a part of it. The big day began with a drizzle and by the time thousands had overtaken the park, the expanse of lawn was trampled muddy and the skies poured a steady sheet of gray rain.

President Reagan's mood was sunny, though, and he opened with, "This is almost as big a crowd as an Osmond family reunion."

Hooper Park erupted with laughter. His politics matched our own, and we were glad to have helped in a small way. We soon received a letter signed by the President. It said in part, "I was particularly delighted to learn of the generous and able assistance you provided on my behalf. You have my deepest appreciation for the support for your contribution to the success of my trip." Jim got a kick out of saying, "Crappers are my claim to fame."

The letter also included an invitation to personally meet the President in Salt Lake City with a small contingent of Utah supporters. Two Canadian kids without a pedigree meeting the United States President? The night before, I was so nervous I turned the words over and over in my head, "Good morning, Mister President. How nice to meet you."

When the President came out, we were surprised by how tall he was, and just as nice as he seemed on television. When we stepped forward, Jim stood by the podium and Ronald Reagan shook Jim's hand while giving him a recognition plaque. Later, we were invited to the White House for a private tour and the President greeted our group. After he and the First Lady left, we got to mill around the room. Jim stood at the Podium, pretending to deliver a presidential speech. We felt like children playing grown-up.

When we returned home, we planned a trip to see my mum. Mum had been diagnosed with cancer and I needed to visit. In the hospital, I brought her a framed picture to place bedside, and she got such a kick out of telling the staff that her daughter met the U.S. President. We sent another copy to Aunt Jean and Uncle Jack who put it in their dining room. The cousins told us Aunt Jean and Uncle Jack paraded guests through the house to show their Kier family wall, always pointing to that picture.

For Halloween that year, I circulated a flyer for a party at work. I bought a little tiger costume with a tail and ears to be worn with tights. I thought it was cute, and Jim got into the spirit by purchasing some vampire teeth. At the office, I removed my jacket and strode down the hallway, then found nobody else in costume. Talk about feeling silly. I made everyone promise to dress up the next year and Halloween became a big holiday for us. Later, Jim got in on the action, too, coming as a hippie or a pirate, but every year he wore the same vampire teeth: vampire hippie or a vampire pirate. He kept them in his desk drawer all year long so he'd know where they were the following year.

By this time, Bonnie was a beautiful young woman. She had been working in the office during high school and we made her start at the very bottom doing dead filing, making copies, and being the front receptionist. She learned fast, and before she graduated, Jim talked to her about going to college. She enrolled right away. As Jim had done with each of the boys, he took the opportunity to talk about her unique potential.

"Bonnie, you have a born knack for figures. You can hold numbers in your head like nobody's business." She got a job with Kay Bowen and Associates, the accounting firm that did our auditing and rented offices in our building. Later as an adult, she got in the habit of pinching her dad on the butt in the office.

We loved seeing her puzzle over a problem and running permutations in her head until the error caught her eye. Bonnie earned her own reputation not working for us, honing her craft from mentors outside of her parents. It was much the same way the boys had grown their skills by working on crews.

Bonnie eventually came to work for Jim as the controller and ran the accounting department for Kier Property Management. Jim and Bonnie spent many hours inspecting properties and reviewing financial records of all the Kier businesses to see how they were doing. Bonnie learned Jim's style of "management by wandering" (MBW), walking around the office and talking with employees. He formed deep relationships and kept a pulse on operations this way.

She moved up the ladder to be Regional Property Manager, Chief Financial Officer, and eventually as President of Kier Management Corporation. She cherished time spent learning from her dad, and Jim felt the same way about mentoring her.

Later, she and I took a hiking class at Weber State together, and she, Steve, and I signed up for 150-mile bike race to raise money for the American Lung Association. Steve ended up driving a support truck when he had to undergo knee surgery, a way for him to encourage Bonnie and I to finish, which we did.

In late 1983, a group of us including Marie met for lunch again at The Horse. We met Wild Bill Wood in the parking lot. His ponytail had grown longer and he had on a pale suit made from flour sack material, with the printing still on it.

Jim gave him the once over and asked, "What's with the getup?"

Bill grinned, "It's my sackcloth and ashes look. Do you like it?"

Jim raised an eyebrow, "That refers to a Hebrew custom..."

Bill raised his hand, "Much as I appreciate the history lesson, we've got work to do."

Inside, we settled into chairs with polished backs like the cantle on an English saddle. Jim's hair looked like soldiers trying to defect, so I ran my fingers through it, and he instinctively brushed my hands aside then shook his mane free. It was one of those routines a couple will repeat thousands of times.

The agenda was to discuss a joint development project: the old Weber Club mansion on 25th Street that we had all fallen in love with. It had been built by LeRoy Eccles in the Prairie Style by a protégé of Frank Lloyd Wright, and had housed the Weber Club for many years. Now it was prime for a renovation into a project we would call The Territory Restaurant. I would work with architect Don Fredrickson and got to choose every detail for a rich period feel.

Jim joked about the project being high-brow for his tastes and Bill ribbed Jim, "I hope you remember your poor friends when this takes off."

Then Jim became thoughtful. "When I was a kid, I never imagined I would set foot in a house like that, let alone own one." He became distant and then he opened up in a rare way.

"I was a janitor at my school. After my grandmother died, they placed me with another family. The system required that I earn a dollar a day for my keep, so they got me this job. I didn't want anyone to know, so I waited in a stall with my feet on the john until the other kids left."

I had never heard that story before.

The table fell silent and I could almost see Jim stitch up the opening he had created in himself. He slid into a half-grin and slipped into his brogue for a joke. Right before the punchline, Jim's face cracked and he could stand it no longer; a wheezing snort of laughter burst out. His eyes welled with tears and his whole body shook, making everyone wait. He tried to compose himself, but everyone else was laughing, too.

He finally delivered the punchline and with everyone in stitches.

Bill whispered to me, "What was the punchline?"

I shook my head, "No idea."

We were still jovial as we emerged as if from a train tunnel into noonday sunlight.

1983

SCOTLAND

———◼———

In 1983[1] when the twins were 14 and Bonnie 19, we saved up to take all three to Scotland for two weeks. Jim contacted the attorney in Scotland who was managing the small estate remaining from Jim's great grandfather, the money that had been helping to support his mother all these years. His name was Bill Anderson and he revealed that his firm holds onto collections from Falkirk historical estates, including original documents from Thomas Kier. We corresponded by letter and he was very gracious about pulling the archives.

On the plane, Jim fidgeted, then went quiet for long stretches. He seemed like an adopted child on his way to meet a birth parent, hoping for a connection to who he was. Would this place feel foreign or familiar? Would a sense of Scottish kinship be revealed? Would he gain a better understanding of what it is to be a sapling from a tree that is still rooted in ancient soil? Still, what if there was no feeling at all, a letdown of sorts? I was also excited about the trip, being half Scottish myself, but it was different for Jim. I knew who my family was.

On top of the personal mission, this trip played to his bookish passion for history, and Jim had studied up. Before Scotland, however, we would explore London. Our plane landed in drizzly gray weather and we spent a few days hitting tourist spots. After that, we boarded the *Flying*

---

[1] *Note: This chapter combines several trips to Scotland. For brevity and the story's flow, these similar trips were combined.*

Scotsman locomotive, considered the world's most famous train, and disembarked inside the grand and bustling Glasgow station wearing California cottons and miniskirts. Locals in heavy woolens and scarves made us feel like we had arrived from outer space. It was June, but hardly summer in Scotland and our American fashion stood out in a concourse where time-darkened bricks and overcast weather hinted toward classic, muted attire. I felt a little ridiculous, but never mind. We stood on Scottish land for the first time.

We rented a car and drove to an amazing hotel with the entrance and lobby built in the thirteenth century. The front desk provided what they believed to be excellent service by placing the girls into the old part with curving stone walls, while Jim and I had the more comfortable but nondescript modern section. I think we all secretly wished the arrangement had been reversed because for the girls, the cold corridors seemed ominous and they huddled together in their room, while we were thrilled at the history that seeped from every wall.

Cousin Jimmy Robertson and his life partner Jimmy (we called them "The Jimmies") had arranged much of the visit for us since they traveled there earlier and had a friend in the travel business. We stayed in very nice accommodations, and in one hotel they saw we were from Utah and asked if we knew Donnie and Marie Osmond, who had just stayed there. The staff told us about having to repair front door glass where fans had rushed the place. Our girls thought that was cool, but we did become aware that the establishments the Jimmies recommended generally targeted an older audience, a bit stodgy for teenage-girl tastes. Still, I smiled and enjoyed how nice they were because if I had booked them, Jim might have grimaced at the cost. Cousin Jimmy got away with it, though.

In one hotel, we got talking with some fellow travelers. When the subject turned to occupations, we mentioned that we had recently remodeled a home on the historic register into a restaurant. They asked its age, then they laughed at our answer. "Why that's just a baby! This building is from the fifteenth century."

We wanted to see everything we could in two weeks, so we ventured from site to site across the green-carpeted countryside. Jim educated us about battles and who defeated whom. The area outside Falkirk had been the northern boundary of the Roman Empire and remnants of the Antonine Wall are still there. Even the weather in that country seems old: rain that greens the green and then seeps into slate-colored rivers. Everything is washed in a mild chill, which in turn is warmed again with northerly sunlight. The cycle repeats century after century.

At our first castle, we explored with hunger to take in all that happened in such a place, reading the placards and asking questions. At the second, we spent a little less time. One was named Kier Castle and we had high hopes of learning about family ties, but the owners knew nothing of the Kiers. Scotland was in recession and people came to own castles looking to eke out a living from tourists. They often lacked historical knowledge or familial connection, and that was the case at Kier Castle.

By about the eleventh castle, Kimi finally spoke up for all three girls, "Dad, I'm going to puke if I see another castle."

We conceded the point, "Okay, enough for one trip."

Jenny and Bob visited Bob's company headquarters in England and then met up with us in Newcastle near the Scottish border. We woke up ready to find where Jim's grandfather had his ale business. Luck shined, and we found the very pub where he had operated. What a feeling to step into an establishment where Jim's family had filled green bottles labeled with the Kier name. We still have one in our possession, and to know where it came from, and where Jim came from, was quite a feeling.

Over frothy glasses, the server told us about the area and motioned behind the building, "This is all subsidized housing."

Bob raised his eyebrows and said, "That is fitting."

After seeing the town, we headed back into Scotland, in very chilly weather. We stopped for gas and as I shivered in my seat, I contemplated Jim's grandparents. They were such a promising couple. They had Jim's mother, Dorothy, in 1911, and Aunt Jean within a couple of years. It must have felt so hopeful then. Their dreams were not to bloom, however, when his health failed and she was left alone with two young daughters. Grandmother's lot would never be an easy one, but she became the rock and the love upon which Jim's childhood was built.

Jim jumped back in the car and I pulled my jacket tighter. He announced, "I know where I want to go for our next vacation."

My mind drifted to tropical beaches when Jim clipped that day-dream like a spent rose.

"Iceland!"

My toes felt like Iceland and I said, "You're crazy."

But he went on, "I'm serious. I have been reading and it's a fascinating place."

We were finally off to Falkirk, the main place of Jim's ancestry. An inscription of the town's motto still makes me smile, "Better meddle wi' the (devil) than the bairns o' Falkirk." I knew it. A little bit of hell in Jim, too. Meddling aside, it is known as one of Scotland's most beautiful towns surrounded by undulating hills, deciduous forests, and tributaries large enough to ferry freight. The panorama is a juxtaposition of green and stone, of rich earth and watery air. Rock outcrops lay above agricultural lowlands that serve as natural foundations, morphing into fortress walls that loom strong over the valleys.

We strolled through the town square paved in herringbone brick and admired Victorian era establishments built toward the end of Thomas Kier's life, when prosperity accelerated in Falkirk. Pausing in the shadow of an unpretentious church bell tower that presided over the square near where Thomas Kier operated his grocery, we pondered what life might have been like then.

This area had served as the cradle of Britain's Industrial Revolution, the heart of a great ironworks machine. By the time Jim's great grandfather finished his term as Provost, a new railway had been established and Falkirk became the first town to install an automated street-lighting system. Falkirk was neck-deep in in the transition from an agrarian society to an industrial one and people moved from the countryside for jobs. Services strained to keep up and resentments sometimes brewed among a new class of urban poor. A Provost had his work cut out for him.

Bill Anderson's law firm was in a centuries-old building with Victorian wood details. Bill was a tall, distinguished looking gentleman in his 60s with salt and pepper hair, a warm handshake, and broad smile. He was wearing a nice suit, although somehow the Scottish brogue gave him a more approachable manner than a similarly educated man in England. He welcomed us into a conference room befitting an attorney in the

United Kingdom. He exuded hospitality and offered to be of whatever assistance he could.

After pleasantries, he filled us in on research he had done. He opened a book on the history of Falkirk and read aloud about Thomas Kier, "He was one of Falkirk's most famous and respected sons who made great strides towards improving the town sanitation, lighting, and policing."

Mr. Anderson took out reference to the official *"Falkirk Archives, Estate, Family and Personal Papers."* This book had the following description:

Thomas Kier Collection
Thomas Kier was Provost of Falkirk from 1857 to 1867. He was born in 1811 in Roberts Wynd and died at his home, Newlands, on the Carse in 1890. He…took up trade as a grocer and was still working into his old age at his High Street shop. He had a brief spell as a Councillor…which culminated in the passage of the Falkirk Police and Improvement Act of 1859. He was Provost for 9 years; he left office in 1867 and was rewarded with accolades and the usual expensive silver plate. During his time the town's general condition improved greatly especially in sanitation, lighting and policing…He was in many ways responsible for the building of the Poorhouse in High Station Road (1857)…"

I was curious and asked, "A poorhouse?"

Mr. Anderson explained, "Scotland had a socially advanced system of poor relief, considered the best in Europe. Falkirk built quarters for the infirm and mentally ill. The poorhouse kindly cared for the indigent and housed them." I thought, *uncanny.*

Mr. Anderson continued, "Your great grandfather was a most compassionate man. More on that in a moment." Then he then touched the archive index again and said, "He is interred in the cemetery it references here," and continued reading:

"…and was in many ways responsible for building of the poorhouse in High Station Road (1857) and the new Cemetery in Camelon…. Around 1850 he purchased a farm in Denny called Linns and thereafter styled himself Thomas Kier of Linns."

Then he looked up and asked, "After this, shall we venture to the cemetery that he helped build? I have the general whereabouts of his marker."

We were eager, of course, but first the main entrée. Mr. Anderson excused himself to the archives and was gone for some time. I imagined catacombs with artifacts ensconced in stone, but it was probably a modern storage room with metal racking. An assistant opened the door because Mr. Anderson needed both hands. He held a heavy metal box about two feet wide, maybe 18 inches deep and 8 inches tall. On the front, formal script in gold ink read, "Thomas Kier of Linns Trust." On the upper corner, the law firm's file number had been painted in quick brush strokes: B31. This box had been in the silent employ of Jim's family for more than a century and our hearts quickened, like deep-sea divers spotting a bona fide treasure chest.

We surveyed the beauty of a patina so dark and unblemished that it obscured the original alloy. Bronze, maybe? We wondered how it might have looked when purchased shiny from a local tradesman, then kept in a store-room or study where Thomas Kier maintained his business accounts.

I imagined that a man who purchased a deed box like this took pride in maintaining a tidy establishment and doing business the right way. Metal casing would protect against fire, it was large enough for a businessman's needs, but not so large as to invite clutter. The fancy lettering on front was a nod to esthetics.

Mr. Anderson placed the box before Jim and said, "It is my great pleasure to present the records of your great grandfather's estate. They show the kind of man Thomas Kier was." We had goose flesh as if Thomas Kier's spirit appeared before us. Jim's fingers trailed the edges, like a birthday boy contemplating how to open a beautifully wrapped package.

Jim opened the box and we noticed a few pinholes had rusted through on top, and the light hinted at coppery tones on the inside lid. There lay heaps of ledgers, receipts and correspondence. Jim's hands gingerly delved in, like a grandparent about to pick up a newborn.

There would not be time to go through everything then, but the box was ours to take home and pore over at leisure. Mr. Anderson commentated on what was before us.

"These ledgers document a good and honorable life. They show groceries sent home with widows to feed hungry children. Thomas Kier must have known they would never be repaid." At this revelation, my eyes welled with tears and the thought of Jim's office where Marie kept a private set of ledgers, tucked away on a shelf for this same purpose.

We craved spending hours, but still wanted to see the cemetery in daylight. We followed Mr. Anderson to his car and he navigated through old, winding streets to the cemetery. Then we snaked across damp grass to the quadrant noted on a little slip of paper. The place felt not unlike the oldest parts of the Ogden City cemetery, both in age and atmosphere. Coniferous trees lined driving paths and headstones were like ones found in other well-kept cemeteries of Europe or North America, those established in the mid-nineteenth century.

It was altogether a different experience than when we had once tracked down a cemetery where the last Jessimans had been interred in the 1950s. There, spindly weeds scratched at our knees and a decrepit groundskeeper's dwelling made one speculate of a town drunkard who had long neglected maintenance duties. Most of the grave markers were eroded and illegible, as if the families had years ago lost track of the past. That graveyard had a spooky vibe, but this was a lovely display of community pride.

Once in the general vicinity, we set about looking for Thomas Kier's marker, which proved rather difficult. We paced the rows, looking and looking, but had no luck. We spread out and doubled back. After quite some time, hopes began to sink that we might leave luckless. Then Mr. Anderson began to laugh aloud.

"Problem is we were looking down and our heads should have been up in the airrrr." He pointed his chin upward and motioned to a very large stone monument. "Hidden in plain sight. So conspicuous we missed it."

Jim and I walked over, then stood silent for a long time. A solemn feeling settled on us, a feeling that mixed awe with curiosity at the very place where DNA connected Jim to the past. A public monument honored this life.

Thomas Kier was born in 1811 and passed away in 1890 at the age of 79. His wife Annie was 24 years younger. We studied the names and I pondered the impossibility of his wife bearing eleven children in total. Then I startled, and tears welled up in my eyes.

Jim asked, "What is it?"

I could hardly find words, "Four babies in little coffins. How could a mother bear it?" Four of their children had died before reaching adulthood.

Mr. Anderson nodded, "Death darkened every door. Childhood diseases stole prince and pauper the same."

Following that sojourn, we made plans—on another day—to track down the old homestead. Mr. Anderson told us that the original home was standing. That was big news! He explained that it had been a bountiful farm, providing his family with means in addition to the shop in town.

Tracking down the site would be the ultimate, and with a little luck we might get up close. Everyone in Scotland had been so welcoming that we were hopeful. With directions scribbled onto a paper and map in hand, we set off into the countryside. The adventure took the entire day. We followed directions, then veered off course and had to maneuver around, missed a turn and doubled back.

We passed a farm for sale and Jim said, "Norma, did you write down that number?" I almost clobbered him with my purse.

We turned onto a side road, which took us several miles until we knew we must have either missed it or were on the wrong road entirely. Sometime after five in the afternoon, we found it. A home much newer than one Thomas Kier would have built stood there, so we weren't sure. I eyed a dozen chunky sheep with soft black eyes and ecru fleece dotting the property. Hundreds more stood grazing farther out. We pulled over and briefly conferred. Should we bother the family to ask? After coming all that way, we had to try.

The homeowners opened their arms and invited us into a formal living room with tasteful décor and flocked wallpaper. Then the wife excused herself into the kitchen for tea and scones. The father called in his children: two big adolescent boys with curly Raggedy Andy hair and twin toddlers with the same red locks. The father explained that he'd kept the older boys home from school that day for branding season. They had about 300 sheep to round up, count, and mark. We could certainly appreciate how much help two teenage boys were.

Over tea, they apologized for not knowing more about the farm's history and were unsure whether their land was the same size as when Thomas Kier had owned it. The family had been told that the original home must have been splendid for its day with frescoes painted on the inner walls.

"But of course, this house was built much later." One historical tidbit they did know was that during the First World War, all the farm's horses—along with everyone else's—had been confiscated for the war effort.

They then asked, "Would you care to see the old ruins?" Of course we did, although the sound "ruins" did not bode well.

Out back, a stone box of an outbuilding with a newer sheet metal roof was being used to store sheep feed. Still standing, yes, but not quite as we had imagined. They walked us through the old home, or what was left of it, and told us how it must have been situated, including a big kitchen area that would have served as the center of family life. Although it wasn't as intact as our imaginations had hoped, a stillness settled upon us. We were standing within walls where Thomas and Annie Kier raised their family and the first James E. Kier would have toddled across the hearth or come dragging in rabbits from a teenage hunt. We hardly had words to express our gratitude at this family's spontaneous hospitality.

We came home with a whole bag full of film canisters to be dropped off at Inkleys, and a metal box that documented shopkeeper transactions, the holdings of an estate, and quill signatures from hands long still. After so much to take in, we would process the revelations for years. What struck me most was the strength held within the Kier name. There was a time before we were married that Jim worried about having children, fearful that they might inherit his mother's fragility. He couldn't have been further off the mark.

Above: Jim's grandmother Jenny Kier with her two daughters: Aunt Jean on the left and Jim's Mum Dorothy on the right

Right: Jim's grandmother Jenny holding cousin Sheila. Front: cousin Joan. Back: Jim

Above:
Norma's mum
Jean on the right;
twin sister, Aunt
Betty who went by
"Auntie Betts," on
the left

Left:
Norma's dad
Norman Jessiman
at age 15
delivering Western
Union telegrams

Above:
Jean and Norman "Jack," Jessiman just before he went off to World War II in 1943. (Norma's mum and dad)

Right:
Norma with her mum and dad

Left:
"Dutchess"
Norma
at about age 3

Below:
Jim at about age 4

Above:
(L-R): Jon, Bob, Norma and
Barbara "Barb"
Jessiman

Right: Jim at about age 16

Top left:
Norma during the time of
the Miss Eskimo contest.

Above:
Jim at Oakwood Collegiate
in Toronto

Left:
Jim and Norma on the street
in Edmonton

September 1, 1956 in Edmonton, Alberta Canada

Left:
Scott on the
left and Steve
on the right

L-R: Bonnie, Norma holding Kara and Kimi, Scott and Steve

Clockwise from bottom left: Kara, Norma, Jim, Scott, Bonnie, Steve, and Kimi. 1985

25th Wedding anniversary trip in Jackson Hole, Wyoming

With President Ronald Reagan in Salt Lake City, 1983

Scott (left) Steve (right)

Kara, Kimi and Bonnie

Hang gliding in Queenstown, New Zealand at ages 65 and 61
Above: Jim
Below: Norma

Jenny and Bob Ross, Norma and Jim in Brentwood Bay, BC

Jon, Barb, Norma and Bob Jessiman
Taken in Vancouver shortly before Bob passed away

Right:
Norma and Jim
outside in the
yard, 2001

Below:
Christmas after
the boys shaved
their heads.
L-R: Scott,
Kara, Bonnie,
Norma, Jim,
Steve and Kimi

Christmas at the cabin, 2015
L-R: Kimi, Bonnie, Kara, Norma, Steve and Scott

L-R: Bonnie, Kara, Norma and Kimi in Scotland, 2009

Above: Steve's family
Back L-R: Jaxon Kier, Kenzie Craven, Logan Clark, Rylee Kier, Riley
Nichols, Abbie Nichols, Tammy Kier, Norma Kier, Steve Kier,
Avery Craven, Bailee Gacioch, Stephen Gacioch
Front L-R: Aiden Craven, Beckem Craven

Scott's family L-R: Scott, Lora, Jason, Karlie, and Carson

Above: Bonnie's family L-R back row: Gage Herrick, Ryan Herrick, Jaden Herrick, Sam Herrick, Bonnie Kier-Herrick, Steve Herrick, Sean Herrick. Second row: Carter Herrick, Misty Herrick, Sophia Herrick, Ivy Herrick, Kayli Rivera, Sean Rivera. Front row: Gavin Herrick, Cole Rivera, and Bennet Rivera

Left: Kimi's family clockwise from bottom left: Alex (in front), Austin, Kimi, Pat, and Ashley

Kara's family clockwise L-R: Skyler, Mike, Kara,
Kailen and Cami (front)

1983 - 1990

MIDDLE AGE

———◼———

After an energetic trip, we slept on the flight and it was good to get home. We plunged back into the work and after returning, Burrell remarked, "Jim has more energy at the end of a workweek than after a vacation."

Jim overheard and piped up, "It's because this woman wears me out!"

Burrell responded, "I can see that, but Jim Kier is the only person I know who recharges *because* of the work, not despite it."

We opened the Territory Restaurant to media fanfare and community hoopla. We were so proud of the renovation and I loved every minute I got to be inside. Then it lost money and never recovered. Liquor costs skyrocketed and we discovered that Ogden was just not ready for a fine dining restaurant. Another painful lesson: stick to the business you know. We had hired a manager and later learned that employees were nipping at the bar and serving too many free drinks. By the time we got a handle on it, it was too late.

Jim called Wild Bill in. "I've hoped to never steer you wrong, but in my estimation, the Eccles home and The Territory were a mistake." Jim showed Bill the numbers with some exit options sketched out, "There's no sense throwing good money after bad."

In the end, we found a guy with a piece of ground he considered a white elephant, and traded his for ours. Jim and Bill went back to our proven playbook. We announced closure of The Territory in February of 1984, the week after we received a national award for its restoration and remodeling. What a big fat disappointment that project had been.

Even with a flop every now and again, life was good in those years and our investments were paying back overall. Jim was ready for one of the very few great splurges of his life. Bob helped Jim choose a beautiful

46-foot sailboat that could comfortably sleep eight. We christened her the Highlander and rented a slip in Oakland, California, so we could enjoy sailing with Jenny and Bob, who had sailed for years. In April, hundreds of decorated sailboats parade for the annual Opening Day on the Bay, a celebration dating back to 1917. As we were out on the Bay and passed a boat that looked a bit stodgy, doctor types or something, Bob emerged with a box of water balloons and began chucking them. He and Jim sent Jenny and I below deck to refill our supply shouting, "More ammo! More ammo!"

When it got choppy, Jenny wrung her hands, but was ever the good sport. When we anchored safely in a languid lagoon she said, "Now this is how I like to sail." Later in Sausalito, we docked at a restaurant.

Over dinner, Bob ribbed Jim, "I still don't know why Norma didn't marry me. I was the best man, after all." It was a line from Bob's repertoire of teasings, but this time Jenny quipped something witty back and we were all in stitches.

After such a good meal, we felt like a stroll in town, but by the time we snaked our way back, the restaurant was shuttered, blocking access to our boat. Oh no! Jim and Bob paced on the beach and huddled before emerging with a plan to scale the gate. They eventually got over, but not without bringing down a drainpipe. I'm glad that was before the days of security cameras on every building corner.

During the first few outings on the boat, Jim and Bob sailed it alone, but before long Jim came to his senses.

"Hell, I bought this thing to enjoy," so we hired a skipper.

Jim had a lifelong love of two main sports: skiing (including water skiing on Pine View dam in Ogden) and sailing. Having an expert on the Highlander relieved him from the stress of being in charge, a little like how he would call Steve to drive our boat to the dam. Now, out on the Bay with somebody else giving orders, we could spend three days at a time relaxing. There is no more restful sleep than gently rocking in a sailboat, especially after a day in the sun. With Jenny and Bob, we never had to put on the dogs, or talk about work or politics. This break from life, with our best friends, let us return to work fully refreshed. I really believe that the older you get, the more you value friends from when you were young.

Back at home, the twins entered center stage with full teenage personalities. They were beautiful young women who got straight A grades through high school and Kimi graduated 11th in her class. Jim drove them to Bonneville High each morning, often getting lost in thought before the twins snapped him out of it, "Dad, you missed the turn again."

Kara had an artistic flair, so she and Jim bonded over a love of art. She honed a natural talent as a clothing designer, sketching original designs in books and learning the whole process. She would not hesitate to spend her entire clothing budget on a single dress if it struck her fancy. Kara was the more outgoing of the two at that age, but as I have mentioned earlier, from the time Kimi was born, she has been an initiator of fun and laughter within the family and business.

In college, they both pursued marketing degrees, each with a unique take on it. Kara pursued design and became a talented graphic artist, while Kimi focused on marketing strategy and had a true knack for sales. Now as an adult, Kimi's outward confidence had blossomed and she emerged as Jim's sidekick at work, a master networker and very good speaker.

During those years, they got to travel with us in the kind of comfort the boys had never known. We loved bringing them places with us and it felt like they kept us young.

Most of our vacations with the kids had been to Canada, peppered with a few more exotic destinations. We visited Aunt Jean and Uncle Jack in Toronto as often as we could. Each time Aunt Jean would show us any new framed pictures she had put up of our family in her dining room.

On one trip, when the twins were still in elementary school, we decided they should meet Dorothy. She had a Barbie doll to give each of them and they were delighted at the gift, although a little confused about who she was and why she didn't seem right. It was the only time they met her. While in Canada that time, we went with the Barbie theme and bought them a sprawling Barbie ranch, which they spread out in the unfinished basement of our new and final home. Eventually they had Barbie cars, Barbie houses and the ranch, a veritable Barbie Town for a whole pack of neighborhood girls who swarmed in like when Park City fills with glam during Sundance.

Later we took the girls and Scott to the Calgary Stampede and also on a guided horseback adventure in Banff. The twins, Bonnie, and I planned all our cute outfits, and then ended up nearly freezing and layering with every article we had brought. It was quite the fashion statement. The girls protested at having to forego hairspray, deodorant, or any form of perfume—bear country rules. They cleaned up in the river, and Kara "accidentally" knocked Kimi in. They ended up having a pretty good time, partly because the male guides flirted with them nonstop, one of whom rode all the way back into town to fetch a six pack of Diet Coke.

When Kimi and Kara were young adults, we got an invitation to a reunion of the old Gang in Britannia. We had attended a first reunion when Scott was 18, and he went along with us. It turned out that the venue was short-staffed at the bar so they roped Scott into working as a bartender for the evening, big-time duty for a Utah kid. For the subsequent trip Bonnie was attending Weber State and could not get away, so we only brought the twins along. We really looked forward to having the girls see our hometown. We stayed at Connolly Acres, where the twins blew fuses in Aunt Jean and Uncle Jack's home by operating hair dryers and curling irons simultaneously.

On the night of the reunion, we all got dressed up and although Kimi and Kara were good natured about it, they were probably not all that excited about spending the evening with a bunch of old people. We could hardly wait, though. There must have been 50 of our friends there, and the moment we entered it was a chorus of "Jimmy and Dutch!"

We introduced the twins, and I overheard one of the girls say to the other, "Ya know, Mom and Dad look pretty good for their age." We got an award for coming the farthest distance.

After a half hour or so, Jim said to our daughters, "I have a surprise." We went outside where a limo waited.

Jim said, "This is for you. Go for it!"

Kara looked at him and said, "You are the coolest dad in the universe!"

They ran toward the limo and waved "bye!" ready to be chauffeured around Ottawa, with the driver to trail them into clubs or anywhere they wanted to go. Jim gave them enough leash to have fun, but made sure they were safe. They talked about it for years.

In 1985, Scott was the first of our children to get married, to the lovely Lora. They have been wonderful partners and their union gave us our first grandchild in 1987. We were just delighted to welcome this smart, beautiful woman into our crazy family and we couldn't be more blessed that they chose each other.

When we became grandparents, it was truly life changing. I remembered how awkward Jim first felt when we had Steve because he had never been around babies, but by the time we had grandchildren he was an old pro. He adored them and so did I. As with each of our children, we always tried to spend as much individual time with each grandchild as possible.

In 1986, the boys were itching for independence, so Jim and I loaned them $300,000 to run Kier Construction as their own company. We would continue to run Kier Management, which we formed back in 1976.

Scott and Steve owned Kier Construction as equal partners and they would alternate turns as President/Vice President every other year with Steve taking the lead first. The two were 25 and 27, energetic and headstrong. Their own word for it (later) was cocky.

That first year, the boys worked their guts out and parlayed $300,000 of working capital into $5.2 million in revenue. They had the world by the tail and finished the year wondering if they would ever top it. They did.

Jim kept close tabs on them, at first dictating that they punch a time clock (which they ignored as ridiculous, and it was). He helped them put out quite a few fires, and he also made sure Margo assigned Kier Construction their portion of whatever expenses came along. She would sometimes raise an eyebrow, "Why are you charging *that* to the boys?"

He'd get this sly look, "They're sitting pretty. It shouldn't come too easy."

Their voracious appetite for growth reminded me of them as teenagers at the fridge during football. Soon they outpaced how quickly we could develop new projects. Jim got a little irritated when they bid on jobs for third-party developers. He clung to a belief that we should keep as much as possible within our family of companies and ensure a liveli-hood for our own. He also hoped they would continue the legacy of government projects and single-family homes, which is precisely why they went after anything but. Instead, they wowed the commercial mar-ket: diversifying into building everything from beautiful car dealerships to credit unions to industrial buildings like those at Thiokol.

When Jim saw the boys toying with ambitious projects for other developers, he went to the employees who he had assigned as scouts for opportunity. He asked them to pull down shelved projects and would walk down the hall to Scott's office.

"I want you to bid on this," he'd say.

Scott would be amused, "I thought you passed this over. What changed?"

Jim would shrug, "My mind."

We did a fun project together when we bought and renovated the Revelle Apartments on 25th and Monroe. Steve liked to point out our former apartment. "I was conceived in lucky #7."

After the first explosive year, the boys had steady growth, with a few ups and downs as they found their rhythm, but always more ups. Jim backed off, or Steve pushed him off. Probably both.

Steve and Scott, who had shared a bedroom their entire time grow-ing up, were as fused together as ever, and they could anticipate the other's moves. They appeared from the outside as singular unity. Like the twins, they were used to people referring to them as one: SteveandScott or "the Kier boys."

Whenever someone realized they had mixed up their names, they just smiled, "We answer to either one."

They began golfing together on Friday afternoons, a ritual almost like date night. Time between holes was enough to resolve any differ-ences from the week. If one got mad, the other made an extra tee time. Golf trips became their getaway.

In about 2008, Steve had a plaque made with a photo of the two on it. They each have one hanging in their office, and the inscription reads:

Golf buddies, business partners and friends.

Most of all, brothers.

In the construction business, there are inevitable disagreements between developers and contractors, and Kier Construction employees knew one was coming when they heard Jim stomping down the hallway. Steve always went toe-to-toe for his own company's profitability, "No, that constitutes a change order," or "Clearly this is the developer's responsibility." Scott stood with Steve until the three reached resolution.

Jim would shake his head, "Those two are as thick as thieves. Thick as thieves."

Subcontractors who worked for us continued with the boys, and in later years, many of their sons would be doing the same. Theron Hill was a superintendent who worked for them maybe ten years and he was a tremendous help in that early time. He and his wife Thora have held a special place in our hearts.

In their second year, Steve became President of the Homebuilder's Association, which meant monthly public speaking. At a big function with hundreds in a ballroom, he got nervous behind the curtain.

He told his friend and mentor Mary Richards, who he called Mom, "I'm gonna die. Look at all those people."

She nudged his shoulder, "Quit being a chicken-shit. Have you ever heard about someone who died from public speaking?" From that point, Steve became the family's designated spokesman. He later served on many boards and foundations.

When the time came for Scott's turn as President, he said, "I'm happier in this role. Steve is good at that, and I am good at this. It's not a competition."

They also decided it would be confusing to have titles change each year, so they kept the status quo but never considered themselves "President" and "Vice President." Rather, they are full partners. I get so choked up whenever Steve acknowledges Scott in speeches.

"Scott is not only my partner, he's my best friend." He can need Scott in a way he could never need his father.

By the third year, Jim backed off considerably. They thought of us as old fashioned, and when they signed the last check to repay our loan, the perforated tearing free from their corporate checkbook felt like their break from us.

Jim commented, "Those two are getting out of hand." There was no stopping them.

On Steve's 30th birthday, an old buddy handed him a surprise. It was a laminated paper, and when Steve studied it, he recognized the old punch list that led to him leaving home. They had a rowdy laugh and Steve hung onto it.

In 1987, Mum's cancer had progressed and we got the call that we needed to get up there as quickly as possible. I caught a flight and I have always felt that she waited for me to get there before going, while Barb and I held each of her hands. It is hard to express how difficult the loss of a parent is, or to measure how much I cried. Mum was 71. Not long after, my youngest brother Bob, who was born with so many health problems, passed at age 46 from a massive heart attack. What a blessing that Mum never had to bury a child.

In 1989, we built some apartments in Richland, Washington, and headed up for the grand opening. It happened to be our anniversary (Labor Day Weekend), so we extended our trip to Victoria and stayed in the elegant Empress Hotel, known for formal high tea. On that trip, our longing for a home in Canada had finally come to fruition and when we saw a townhome development going in, we picked a lot and made a down payment. I spent the next five months flying back and forth to decorate and finish it.

Sometime after the townhome was finished (the following February), we had the Highlander moved up to Brentwood Bay in Victoria not too far from where I was born. When Jim and Bob and crew pulled into its new port, I had a bagpiper playing, which is traditional for good luck. We had hors d'oeuvres and a little celebration.

From that point on, we always had salmon in the freezer at home and often invited family over from Vancouver—or from anywhere in Canada, really—for big salmon barbecues. My only regret was that my parents did not live to see us purchase our first home back in "God's country." I missed the supply of Canadian flags they always brought down on their visits, so it became my job to bring Canadian reminders back for the grandkids, like good chocolate and red double decker buses.

During that trip when we brought the boat up, I had not thought about the weather being chilly, so Jim and I went out walking and I stepped into a little shop with his credit card—I didn't have my own yet. I spotted the most beautiful white Italian leather jacket. The $600 tag dangled like a fishing lure. I circled a few times and on an impulse, charged it up. When I met Jim back on the street wearing it, he said I looked nice.

Then he looked up and asked, "How much?"

I tried to act nonchalant, "Oh, six hundred."

His jaw hit his knees and he huffed, "See what I get for letting you loose with the credit card." I shrugged it off, but did feel a tiny bit guilty. After that I got my own credit card.

Even though I had splurged, he was in a good mood and I looked at my handsome hubby with wind-tousled hair, wearing a buckskin leather vest and signature boots. He was as handsome as the day I met him. No, that wasn't true. He was even better now. This was prime time. I caught his gaze across the table at lunch and held it to say without saying, *We won't need a dresser tonight. Hotel doors lock.*

On our way home, Jim presented a customs declaration and the guard took one glance and started laughing. He called over a buddy and pointed to the paper, "This might be a record for the most honest form I've ever seen."

It itemized every chocolate bar and trinket. The man's integrity was like a laser level. I handed him my form with an estimate of $200 for "miscellaneous souvenirs." I later realized I had crossed the border wearing a $600 Italian leather jacket that I had completely forgotten to list.

During that same period, Jim realized we needed to add a stronger security presence to watch over our apartments and he met Jerry Burnett, who was retiring from Ogden Police Department. We hired him on to patrol our properties, which was the beginning of a great friendship between our families. Jerry and Jim might seem like different personalities because Jerry could be a little gruff, as watchdogs often are, but we could not have asked for a more loyal or protective friend. With Jim's help and encouragement, Jerry started his own business, BRB Patrol. We remained a client from that time forward.

Jerry took his role seriously and would often come in with something like mace for the women in our office, or a lecture about being aware. Jerry sometimes let Jim know about a tenant in need in one of the apartments, because he knew Jim liked to step in and help. Jerry also directed his guys to drive past our home, especially when we were out of town. He became an expert at how to keep drugs and bad elements out of a complex and wanted every family who lived in our units to feel safe.

We held a summer party in our yard each year for the B.R.B. employees, parties for our employees, and parties whenever family visited. Even as a teenager, Bonnie would start getting sleepy, but did not want to be impolite with guests still in the house.

Aunt Jean and Uncle Jack visited to celebrate their fiftieth wedding anniversary. Jean spent as much time in the pool as she could, but Jack generally refused to get in in. That trip, though, Jack finally went off the diving board. It was a big moment. We had the most wonderful time, and it turned out to be their last trip to us together. Not long after that, while we were staying with Jenny and Bob in California, we received word that Uncle Jack was declining rapidly. We got on the first flight back to Salt Lake City and then a connecting flight to Toronto. We were too late, though, to really say our goodbyes. By the time we got there, Uncle Jack was out of it and did not recognize anyone. Jim was devastated. Uncle Jack was the closest to a father he ever had. Steve later told me that when Jim called home to give the news, he was crying.

I'll always remember the wonderful pastor who said in the service, "Jack is not gone. You will see glimpses of him in loved ones: phrases he used, mannerisms, and the lessons he taught us. Watch for these moments and you will see him from time to time."

Within a year or so, Aunt Jean's health began to decline, too. Joan and Sheila brought her to visit us in Brentwood Bay and soaked in the time with her. When she passed away, we had said our goodbyes before the funeral. We have missed her terribly.

1990 - 1998

SCARES AND JOYS

In 1990, we learned of a need in our community, and the fact that there even was a need for it was a haunting thought. Children who were victims of abuse had to go to the police station to be interviewed or to testify, a cold environment. They might have to repeat the story over and over again, possibly in front of large groups of people. Not only did these conditions undermine prosecution, but the emotional toll on tiny victims was more terrible than I could imagine.

Ogden's lead prosecutor and many others decided to do something about it, rallying to propose a new Children's Justice center, a child-centered place for interviews to happen. Those interviews would be conducted by a social worker, sensitive to children's emotions, and trained to not ask leading questions. Jim had been called early on because he was known as an expert with government projects. The Children's Justice Center later moved into a home on 25th Street and we again rallied behind the project, donating remodeling work and my decorating services, and getting subs to pitch in, too. When that project came together, it was a model for other centers around the country.

In *National Real Estate Investor Magazine*, Jim was quoted, "If you take out of the community, then you need to put it back in. That's the way I was raised, and that's the way I've always felt."

Jumping ahead, to 2001, one of our attorneys Jane Marquardt approached us to contribute matching dollars and in-kind contributions toward an even better Children's Justice Center. Jane was donating an elegant and larger home on 24th and Van Buren where her law practice had been located. It had rich woodwork, leaded glass windows, and in the springtime a matriarch magnolia graced the backyard with delicate pink blooms.

So again, Jim oversaw the development, Kier Construction did the remodel, and I decorated. The new rooms had one-way glass so law enforcement could observe the interview without children being frightened by their presence. In the room for young children, I designed a brightly decorated jungle theme with stuffed animals for children to cuddle. Large cushions stacked atop each other so children could sit above eye-level of the interviewer, giving them a sense of empowerment. For the older kids, I made an ocean motif but with a more sophisticated air, evocative of sea breezes. The walls were painted as if sitting on a beach looking toward a lighthouse from white wicker furniture.

The Children's Justice Center said this in an article, "When you visit the Weber/Morgan Children's Justice Center, you sense the presence of our Guardian Angels, Jim and Norma Kier. They cannot be labeled mere supporters; their contributions go far beyond that; they have truly been involved body and soul." We later became strong and lifelong supporters of the Christmas Box House after Kier Construction built it.

In the early 90s, one matter that needed some attention was a bruise on Jim's neck and an Ear, Nose and Throat Specialist said he needed surgery to take care of a nerve that had died. Jim was not happy about this idea, but we scheduled surgery at Lakeview Hospital. While we waited, Jim shifted and paced. After they put the bracelet on Jim's hand, he fidgeted with it and then did a double take. The name wasn't his.

"Let's run for it. They're about to amputate my leg."

The nurse kept apologizing before sorting out the tags and settling Jim down. The surgery went fine, but the routine was for Jim to stay in for a couple of days. I stayed bedside the whole time except at night and as I gathered up my bag, he said, "Get here early. I want *out!*"

On my way out, the nurse said, "Why don't you return about 10 o' clock. That gives us time to dress the wound and give medication."

When I opened the door at ten, he was dressed and sitting up straight, like he had been that way since dawn, "Where have you been?"

I was apologetic, "This is when the nurse told me to come."

But he repeated himself from the night before, "Get me out of here." As unpleasant as that experience was for Jim, I think it gave him

152

a small glimpse into what it was like to be in a hospital, hitting home when others in our work family got ill.

In 1992, health insurance costs were skyrocketing and we had to make a change to keep the premium affordable for our employees. After weighing options, we went from a low deductible to $2,500. That change was made in mid-November and On December 30th, Margo received the worst of news—she was diagnosed with cancer. We were all stunned. She was so fit and healthy, full of energy and fun. It wasn't possible. Not Margo. She took great care of herself. She seemed very, very brave, but it must have been scary.

What everyone in the office must have been thinking, but nobody said, was that Margo had cancer with the new deductible. As the controller, she had been in on the insurance decision, so when it affected her personally, she did not say a word.

We and the other employees rallied, so her emotional support from work was strong, and the next day Jim walked into her office and placed a personal check from us for $2,500. In the coming weeks, he also tracked down any books he could find on the type of cancer she had, signing them "To Margo, from Dad."

In 1993, we were in the middle of another huge HUD project. The Marion Hotel property on lower 25th Street had taken nearly three years of planning and red tape to get to the point of actual mod-rehab because of its location in a historic district, tenants-in-place, and a half dozen agencies with their say. This building was once part of Ogden's bustling downtown with well-appointed rooms. Then in the wild 20s, the famous Belle London ran a house of ill repute in it. By now, lower 25th Street fell into decay and the need for dignified low-income housing was acute in Ogden at that time. In the Royal Hotel, for example, the rooms had no refrigerators, so passersby would look up at the windows and see food jars outside on window ledges during cold weather. Other infrastructure was on the brink and it had the kind of dank hallways that made your skin crawl. After the green light, the boys began the actual rehab.

In every one of these Section 8 projects, our capable staff helped with thousands of details. At the end, Jim's devoted secretary Marie would vow that this would be her last, something like going through natural childbirth. Sometime later, though, we would eye a new building, get baby hungry, and get busy.

In the middle of this project, though, life outside work happened and Marie's father fell ill. She prepared herself for the inevitable and we felt so sorry for her. On one of her days off, Jim picked up the phone and it was Marie's dad.

He said something like, "My time is short, so I won't beat around the bush. You're a good man and have daughters, so I know you'll understand a dying man's request. Will you look after my little girl?"

The weight settled Jim deeper into the chair, "You have my word." Marie's dad passed away the following week. For nearly three decades, Jim kept that promise and did not tell Marie.

A few months after Marie's dad died, she and Jim were working together and Marie screened a call, putting it on a brief hold.

After picking up and speaking into the receiver briefly, he looked up and asked, "Would you give me a minute?" After a while, he waved her in and asked, "Marie, will you reschedule my meetings next week, and get me a flight to Toronto?" He paused, "Dorothy has died."

When Jim told me the news, I said, "I want to be there for you," but he was firm.

"I appreciate your support. Really, though, you don't need to go." I respected his space on this as I always had.

After he flew out, Annette asked Marie, "How did he seem when he left?"

Marie shrugged, "A little quiet maybe. Why?"

Annette answered, "With his mother finally passing, I wondered."

Marie leaned onto the doorframe in a moment of recognition and bewilderment, "Dorothy is his *mother*?"

Annette blinked. Not one of us knew all the layers Jim pushed out of sight under a man's-man jacket of work, humor, and protectiveness.

Marie said, "I thought his mother was gone long ago."

Annette answered, "She was."

Not long after Dorothy's death, Marie came into the office looking frightened.

"Jim, I need to take Monday off. It's my daughter, Rachel. She has a strange pain in her back and they want to run tests. It's fine, I'm sure." But the inflection in her voice was a question, not confidence.

Jim nodded, "Of course. Family first."

On Tuesday, Jim asked, "Learn anything?"

Marie held back tears, "Results aren't in. They're trying not to scare us, but they said the word leukemia."

A few days later, the emotional bomb exploded. Marie's seven-year-old daughter Rachel had leukemia and would undergo treatment at Primary Children's Hospital immediately.

We told Marie, "Take whatever time you need. We'll be here and we'll cover for you." Jim found a book on childhood cancer and signed the inside cover.

Jim walked down to accounting, "Calculate an average of Marie's hours over the past three months. She'll be gone a lot so just pay her the average, regardless of what she works."

God, a child. Marie's seven-year-old daughter in dresses and playing with dolls. And cancer. Like that, one day you're caught up in whether a stack of papers has every signature and date in the right spot, and the next day we're praying for Rachel's life, bargaining with God to let us trade places with a little girl suffering body-slamming treatments and we're aching for parents who face the deepest primal fear: losing a child. Before you become a parent, you just don't know what fear is.

Rachel underwent chemotherapy and we visited quite a bit when it was permitted. One afternoon, Jim noticed a troll doll on her bed and Rachel said, "Trolls are my favorite!" From then on, whenever we passed a toy store or an airport gift shop, Jim made a quick sweep, scanning for trolls. If they had one, he would bring it back to her.

It's a strange thing when someone's life comes to a halt for something like cancer. It feels like the whole world should stop its work, but it doesn't. It never even slows its pace. In this way, the deadlines never stopped for the rest of the staff who did their part to show support by picking up any slack, the same when Margo got cancer. And so, we finished the Marion and the Standard Examiner wrote a nice editorial:

It also signals another successful reclamation project on a building whose vibrancy and functions were dulled by the ages....It will now resume its prominence...re-

built and refinished and give new missions and provide services to Ogden's historic 25ᵗʰ Street District. Ogden developer Jim Kier recognized the serious absence of single-room occupancy hotels. He has shown a keen interest in maintaining the ones already here rather than pursue a course for building new ones…Despite heavy resistance from nearby businesses, Kier has carried out his commitment to upgrade them into safe, decent housing for single people who cannot afford apartment rent…It took three years to get all the approvals to begin the 86-room Marion project with resistance coming from different quarters and carrying the whiff of xenophobia. Eventually, Kier's management won respect.

That November, we started a family tradition by serving a full Thanksgiving dinner to residents of the Marion. We really enjoyed our evening there. Residents told us how much the renovation had meant to them, and how they appreciated small amenities we take for granted. Jim talked easily with them and connected. We continued to serve Thanksgiving dinner each year and after Jim was gone, many of the residents remembered him.

On Christmas Eve, Marie hadn't been in the office for a month, but she said she wanted to meet Jim to finalize some paperwork before the holiday. They caught up about Rachel's progress and Marie thanked him for being so supportive. Later, when she came back, she told Margo, "They never once mentioned my hours."

That brave little girl underwent chemo and responded well to treatment. Each test left us more optimistic and she inched toward a "cancer free" declaration. There isn't a happy enough word to describe the swing from Marie's worst fears to the highest joy when the doctors finally delivered that news. Jubilant. Ecstatic. Grateful. Rachel would fulfill everyone's hopes and grow up to have three children of her own. Her illness showed us what a precious gift a normal childhood is.

Steve remarried on August 5, 1995, and we just thought the world of Tammy, a stunning woman who brought two wonderful children into our family at that time. They had a lovely ceremony by an LDS Bishop, who we learned lived next door to the very first house we built, and remembered us from all those years ago. The two of them would have another three children, and were very well-suited to work together through everything a growing family business would entail.

In 1996, we were busy enough to divide out secretarial duties again and advertised for someone to take over administrative support for the business side of things. Marie had become very, very busy and we had enough work to keep her consumed just on executive secretarial duties. We hired a sharp, slender woman named Connie Sheets who had just moved to Utah.

After she came aboard, she said, "This was the only interview I went on, but it seemed like such a good place, I stopped looking." She was young and nervous about working for Jim at first.

Marie reassured her, "I understand, but he's a really nice man. This family is good to everyone."

Connie's family was in California, and a few weeks later she commented to Marie, "It's like we are their daughters."

Marie said, "That's the Kiers."

Then Connie got married and when she first announced her pregnancy, Jim crinkled his nose saying, "I can't take the news. There are two groups of people that everyone knows don't do *that*." He was laughing now, "…your parents and your children."

After he composed himself, he said, "Congratulations. You'll be a wonderful mother."

Connie confided to Marie, "It's nice to have a second Dad with mine so far away."

Connie started with labor pains at work, and they phoned her husband who could not be reached right away. Jim drove her to the hospital while Marie kept trying to get through.

After checking in, a doctor asked Connie, "Is this your husband?"

She laughed, "This is my *boss.*" And then she clarified, "And let's be clear—he's not the father! My husband's on his way."

When Marie changed her schedule to part time, we tried to hire another assistant, but that girl was something else. She had a belly dancing business on the side and would field phone calls using her stage name.

One afternoon Jim dialed Marie at home, "When are you coming in? I just caught a glance of the temp and she was *posing*."

Marie burst into laughter, "She is totally coming onto you!"

Jim was aghast, "She is NOT flirting. She's just not all there."

Marie was laughing, "Whatever you say, boss." Jim seemed horrified.

By this time, Jim had wrapped up the last details of his mother's estate which included a small inheritance that had originally come from the estate of Thomas Kier, then passed down to the first James E. Kier, and eventually divided between his two children, Dorothy and Aunt Jean. Jim would be the last to receive what amounted to about $13,000 U.S. The news gave us the same feeling as the big metal box; it seemed sacred and Jim wanted to do something special with the money. After mulling it over, he said, "Maybe we could donate it to a children's hospital in Falkirk, something Thomas would have done." *I love you,* I thought, and added another trip to Scotland to our bucket list.

Now Kimi was working in the business full time. She got her real estate license and broker license. She was very young when she got her broker license and she went everywhere she could with Jim, his work sidekick of sorts. Knowing we had been involved with the Children's Justice Center in Ogden, a group from Davis County invited them to a meeting. Upon return, Kimi and I went to lunch and I asked her how it went. She set a bite of Romaine back on the plate and a smile lit up her face.

"We're sitting around a huge table with all these mayors, city reps, and county people and they are lost. Nobody has any direction, and I'm looking at my watch like *'this meeting's gonna go all day.'* Dad lets it run for a bit and then raises his hand. A County Commissioner says, 'Jim, what do you think?' Everybody looks at Dad and the room goes silent, Mum. I'm not kidding. Like *Jim Kier is about to speak.*"

She took a bite, touched a napkin to her mouth and continued. "In five minutes, Dad lays out the whole plan. We do this, and then we do this. Everybody nods like *yep, that's the plan*, and the meeting ends in ten minutes. Dad was in a room of leaders, and he was the leader. He was awesome."

A few days later, Jim took me to see the property that had been donated and I had flashbacks of the Brigham City apartments. It was a turn-of-the-century farmhouse that had been vacant for years. Structural issues gave us pause, and it looked like the wind would blow it over. Jim still made it work, and Davis County ended up with a showpiece Children's Justice Center of their own. That's what Jim did, he made weak structures strong and built places to withstand storms. The boy without a home now built safety for families, children, and those most in need.

On my 60th, birthday we were to attend a Republican Party function, so I dressed in a somewhat conservative dress with Jim looking so handsome in a suit. I was happy that it would be held in the Ben Lomond Hotel.

We entered a packed room, but when we walked in, the room went silent for a moment and then everyone yelled, "Surprise!"

I blushed and whispered to Jim, "If I had known, I would have worn a sexier dress."

Part of the entertainment involved our kids roasting me, payback for all the Christmas mornings I had made them wait while I put on my makeup. Steve also did a great impersonation of me posing whenever a camera points in my direction, a habit from modeling school all those years ago. We laughed and had a wonderful time

To open the dancing, Jim led me onto the wide-open dance floor. He was such a polished dancer, and I twirled and twirled at his lead. The room was otherwise still, just music and our feet with all eyes focused on us. Jim and I had been dancing together nearly 50 years, and it came as naturally as working. That moment sparkles in my memory. Then everyone else flowed onto the floor. When Jim had enough, he said to Scott, "Will you dance with your mother?"

Bonnie was the first of our children to graduate from college. After working in public accounting with Kay Bowen for two years, Jim asked her to come work for him and run his accounting department. He involved her in many meetings with bankers, HUD personnel, and estate planners. Bonnie spent many hours working overtime and on Saturdays with Jim. She enjoyed those days with him, and chose to work on Saturdays just to spend time together. Very often, they would go to lunch at The Horse. They also drove around to properties and Bonnie took notes on what needed to be done.

On August 3, 1996, Bonnie was a stunning bride in a gorgeous dress, a perfect day. During the toasts, Jim picked his way over to the microphone and said, "Steve is better at this, but I have a story. It's a little out of school because I have never told it to anyone, but it's about you, Bonnie."

He turned toward her and brushed his upper lip, "When Bonnie was two weeks old, Norma's mum came down from Canada to help. They went out shopping and left Bonnie with me. While she slept, the phone rang and I went in the other room. Of course there was this big water break and I dashed down there in the car. A minute after being there, I remembered Bonnie, and sped back home. Luckily I beat Norma and her mum back, and Bonnie was still sleeping. They got home and asked how it went. I said, 'Oh yeah, everything's fine.'"

The room erupted in laughter and Jim turned to Bonnie's husband, Steve Herrick, "So you can see that I have been carefully watching over her all these years. Now it's your turn." Steve Herrick is a great guy, handsome and with a tender heart. He brought four wonderful children with him into our family, and they would add two more together.

A month later, on September 1, 1996, we had another big party: our 40th Anniversary in the Weber Club of the Eccles mansion that we had remodeled earlier. Again, friends and family surrounded us, although this time it was more casual. Jim wore a white captain-style shirt with a ball cap and I was in a little sundress. Steve pinged a fork on his glass and stood, turning toward us.

After the room quieted, he said, "You two have accomplished so much in 40 years. But the single greatest thing you ever did for us was…" He paused for a moment, his voice catching, "The single greatest thing was staying together. Let's raise our glasses to celebrate Jim and Norma's 40th Anniversary."

We cut the cake and Bob Ross tried to egg me on, "Stuff it in his face like the old days!" Then it was dancing time. Jim and I boogied together, then Steve, then anybody else who would, and as usual, Scott more than everyone.

As our anniversary present to ourselves, Jim and I took a month's trip to New Zealand and Australia in 1996. Traveling down under had been on our bucket list and this would be a different kind of trip than others with GE or times when we had a big itinerary of everything we wanted to see. Those trips had always been so packed that we would make ourselves late for the next activity if we lingered too long anywhere. This time we had no agenda, we just slept in and did as we pleased, strolling down the sidewalk holding hands. Two such expansive, fascinating countries invited that kind of time. Also, the business was in capable hands while we were away.

While in New Zealand, Jim had the genius idea to go hang-gliding. What were we thinking at ages 65 and 61? They unfolded the dubious contraptions strapped atop a car and I was terrified to get strapped in. What if the wings that seemed like paper folded up like that in thin air? Jim was grinning and I inhaled to channel my inner brave, then clutched my arms around the instructor like a baby with separation anxiety. We took flight over lavish green hills, enjoying the whoosh of wind without artificial sounds.

It was an incomparable thrill, and after a little while the instructor said, "You can let go now. You're strangling me a bit."

I tried to relax on the poor man, but still said, "You're my lifeline!" We landed safely in a field of sheep, exhilarated.

Whenever we traveled into the countryside, I made it a point to book some horseback riding. I just felt a bond with these animals. It was as if we understood each other: each of us feisty at times, but willing to do our part. If I have a totem animal, it might be a deer for quick, light step, but a horse is more likely. Horses work for their keep. Horses even sleep standing up.

When we landed in Australia, we stayed with our old friend from Britannia, Freddie Goodfellow. We had exchanged Christmas cards and kept in touch, but the last time we saw him was when the family stopped on their way to board an ocean-liner, their toy car crammed with belongings like a prairie schooner on their move to Australia.

Although in a wheelchair now and looking thinner, he had the same stubbornness and sense of humor. He was separated from his wife and picked us up from the airport in a vehicle outfitted with hand controls. His apartment was designed with wheelchair-height counters and he hosted in the same fussing way I did in our home. He cooked us spaghetti with meatballs, set the table, and attended to all household duties, but was apologetic about one detail.

"Norma, would you help with putting on the bed linens? I can't reach that far."

The first night, Jim and Freddie stayed up late laughing and telling old stories. I got sleepy, but they were going strong at 2 a.m. when they realized the time difference made it mid-morning in Canada. They compared address books and dialed any of the gang who happened to pick up, joking and having a marvelous time.

Years later, we talked about our favorite trips together. It's funny that after all the amazing experiences we had, that trip—especially our time in New Zealand—shined as the best *vacation*, just the two of us. Simple and spontaneous. That trip filled the soul like we were a young couple again, but somehow better now. We were still so in love after forty years. More in love, actually, a fuller kind.

1998 - 2005
CANCER

—■—

In 1998, Jim got a rash on his neck and went to see our family doctor. We wondered if it might be related in some way to the surgery he had a few years earlier. Doctor King took one look at it and suggested a biopsy. Rather than calling over the phone with results, Dr. King wanted him to come into the office. Jim slipped out to the appointment alone.

When Jim returned to work, he came and got me. Then he closed the door. I don't remember exactly what he said, only that with the word lymphoma I was stunned and confused. What does that mean? Jim was in front of me acting calm.

"I feel great. I'm only 67 and they say I'm in good health. I could live a long time." What? We're talking about *living*?

He tried to reassure me, "With this type of cancer, there's a strong chance something else will get me first." Did he just say the word cancer? Cancer, with a capital C? A flood of tears came over me and he took my hand, trying to calm me down.

"I'm a fighter and there are incredible advances. I know we'll beat this. I know it." Then he rounded up the kids and it was crying time with the girls. When they saw me in tears, it was real for them, and when they started crying, it was real for me, too.

We had a million questions and a follow-up appointment with an oncologist as soon as we could get in. There were more tests to confirm because we wanted to be sure, but the doctors never really had any doubt. In our first appointment, we wanted to know how much of our life had to change, especially with Jim feeling normal at that point.

We had been worried about our GE trip to the Canary Islands coming up, "Do we have to cancel our flight?"

The oncologist reassured us, "By all means go." We were happy at that. Now we had context. If we could travel, we were still living.

Jim had Marie book his doctor appointments like they were planning commission meetings, and he scheduled a lymphoma seminar like it was a homebuilder's conference. He ordered every book title he could track down on lymphoma and when Marie called him in to get the shipment, he waited for the back-and-forth banter. She almost began to speak, and then didn't.

After composing herself, she said, "You'll find the answer in one of these."

Jim's act that nothing was up did make me feel better, and he felt healthy. We made ourselves forget about it except for the lymphoma workshops, which were very sad places to be. Many of the attendees were in the final stages, sleeping during the speakers while their loved ones clutched at desperate hopes. Our situation was different because we were in the beginning stages. Jim was healthy, willing to do any treatment, and new breakthroughs were happening all the time. We came back to work which overrode any will to slow down. Jim never did plan to retire.

Back at home, Kimi began trailing Jim in his political activities. She took on fundraising efforts for Glenn Meacham's mayoral campaign and set up headquarters in a corner of our office with a hand-me-down desk and phone. She had conquered shyness, becoming a fearless fundraiser with just the right amount of grace.

One contributor said, "You are the most well-mannered young lady I have encountered in years."

She said, "My parents expect it."

High-level donors could be elusive and after leaving repeated messages for Dee Livingood of Big D Construction, she was getting exasperated, and then got scheming on a plan. She called his office and left a message that he was to call Jim Kier, figuring he'd return *that* call. When he phoned in, she would just intercept it.

He did call back and Kimi slid over to the receptionist's desk, "Is that Mr. Livingood? Can I just talk to him first?" Jim heard it from the other room and poked his nose around the door, onto the scent of something amiss.

He pressed her and Kimi finally was out with it, "My calls kept getting screened but I figured he would pay attention to you." He decided to have some fun and directed Connie to put the call through to him.

"Dee, my daughter says you won't take her calls." Kimi's cheeks were flushed with embarrassment as Jim emerged and said, "He wants to talk to you."

She picked up and Dee asked with a smile in his voice, "How much?" He directed her to come get a check for the remainder of what she was trying to raise. When Jim and Kimi went to the next campaign meeting, the committee was impressed by her.

By that time, she was also using her real estate license to buy and sell for us. A townhome project in Centerville sold like hotcakes and she was in the middle of selling off another development in South Ogden when she got married to Pat Noar in 1999. As we drove her to the rehearsal dinner the night before her wedding, we passed a commercial property and Jim pulled over.

"Kimi, when you get back from the honeymoon, will you find out how much they want for it?" Kimi and I rolled our eyes, but she wrote it down anyway.

During the father-daughter dance, he leaned in and asked, "How many of the South Ogden homes have you sold?" She laughed out loud, but told him the latest number. He was part joking and part bonding in the language they knew.

Pat is a hard-working and handsome man who later started his own business, and has been a great addition to our family. The two of them have three children together and have made each other very happy through all the stresses of work and family.

Kimi continued going to seminars and homebuilder's conferences with us. While I was filling my bag with flooring and countertop samples, Jim and Kimi went to the temple of books together. The ladies greeted him by name and gave a personal tour of their new offerings.

He told Kimi, "There isn't a problem in the world somebody hasn't written about. I've always found what I needed in a book." She chose a stack for herself and when they checked out, she was a little surprised by the small fortune he had spent.

Kimi and I also slipped out for a while to go shopping. When we brought purchases into the hotel room, Jim snorted a bit, which we knew meant he was miffed. We had frittered away valuable floor time, but he got over it. As nice as the shopping was, the real goal was one-on-one time with Kimi. For that, I will not apologize.

In the airport, she hefted her big suitcase onto the conveyor. Who knew words could weigh so much?

He looked panicked, "You're checking the books?"

She shrugged, "I'm not lugging this across DFW in heels."

His face lost color and, no exaggeration, he looked a little like a wave of the flu had passed over him. "What if they don't make it? What if they get damaged? What if one comes up missing?"

She rolled her eyes, "That's what insurance is for, Dad." People were shifting in line behind us.

"I don't like this one bit," but he relented.

In the Salt Lake airport, he was cagey until he spotted her bag. The moment he had it down, he opened it and demanded an inventory. One book was missing. Had it been stolen? *Oh please,* Kimi's eyes seemed to say. They rifled through the entire bag until they located it wedged between two others and Jim could start breathing again. The next time we traveled, Kimi took our lead and brought a carry-on just for books.

Upon return, UPS had Marie sign for a package. She went to lift it and the driver said, "I wouldn't try. Heavy."

She attempted anyway, then went to get Jim, who lit up like a birthday boy, "My books!"

She looked a little horrified and said, "How *much* did you spend?" Then he recited his speech, "If I get just one thing out of each book, it will be more than worth the price."

Her face said, "Doubtful," but the only words were, "Please find the receipt."

Later, he walked into a staff meeting with books cradled like little darlings. Jim donned his professor persona and passed out books, which were received with all the enthusiasm of a term paper assignment, "I expect these to be read," he said.

Someone groaned and Jim said, "A man is himself plus the books he reads."

In the hallway and out of earshot, Burrell whispered to Steve,

"There is no way in *hell* your dad has read all those books."

Around the time Utah was preparing for the Olympics, we were advised that it would be best for us to seek American citizenship and Canada is a country that lets you keep your original citizenship. So we studied and took the exam, and when we returned to the office, our employees played O Canada and the Star-Spangled Banner and had a cake with flags from both countries. We were absolutely thrilled and it was one of the proudest moments of our lives.

During the Olympics in 2002, we hosted Cousin Joan and her husband Walter and their son, Sean, and cousin Sheila from Toronto. How wonderful to host Jim's cousins from Canada as the world's eyes turned to Utah.

This was a great period for our family. The pool brought our grandchildren throughout each summer and being grandparents was the most rewarding part of family life we had experienced. We attended games and functions and we set up a fund to help any grandchild who wanted to get a college degree. The businesses were doing well and we traveled often. It occurs to me that there are not many details to recount here because the very best times can seem unremarkable to others.

Then Jim began showing signs of illness and we had to face up to treatments. When one has cancer of the blood there are no tumors to remove—it's chemotherapy.

He fidgeted on our way to Ogden Regional, having read perhaps too extensively before being inducted into the chemo club. They rigged him up and he willed himself to sit there for roughly the time it takes to run a marathon. After that, he was spent, and then intense aches and sickness overtook his body.

He went back into the office as soon as he was able, probably sooner, and plopped down at Marie's desk. "Holy shit! They put children through that? I have a whole new appreciation for Rachel, and for what it must have been like to be her mother or father."

I helped Jim pass hours during treatments, and occasionally one of our employees would spell me so I could run an errand. Bonnie often came by, bringing a cookie or a drink and sitting with him for a while.

On a day like that, Marie walked in and he brightened. On his face read not only fondness, but hope that they might not waste the time. If

Marie brought work bedside, it was Jim's equivalent of bringing a troll doll. Mostly, though, they just talked. As they did, he stopped mid-sentence to greet a young man pushing a cart.

A little while later the same orderly passed and again Jim said, "Hello!" The young man seemed to duck and kept on.

The third time, Jim asked, "How are you?" The young man stopped, smiled, and talked easily with Jim before returning to work. While they chatted, Marie noticed the cart had bedpans on it. She thought about how Jim's way was the same whether an oncologist, nurse, or janitor.

Jim took as little time away from the office as possible, even when he was ill. One day, Kimi was working when Connie came over and touched her arm, "You might want to check on your dad. He just got word Freddie Goodfellow passed away."

Kimi asked, "The pilot with nine lives?" Connie nodded.

Kimi tiptoed to the door and peered in for a moment before knocking. Jim's head rested on his palms, fingers deep in hair with a letter before him.

"He's weeping," she whispered to herself. It was the first time she had ever seen her father's defenses come down. Part of her felt relieved to know he could cry, and the other part ached to dry his tears. She tapped softly on the doorframe. He looked up, startled and straightening up.

"I'm sorry. You shouldn't see this," as if it was a burden on her.

She reassured him, "Don't be, Dad. A good friend is worth tears."

He nodded, "That he was." She rested her hand on his shoulder, not sure what else to do. They lingered together until he willed the tears into hiding and reached for a stack.

She turned to leave, "I love you Dad." He nodded, and his eyes seemed to retreat in memory. She heard papers shuffling to mimic work. It was the only time she ever saw her dad cry.

One afternoon, Jim took Kara to The Horse, just the two of them. That day, she felt like a buddy, as if she were hanging out with Jimmy from Ottawa. Her dad was relaxed and jovial in this everyman's bar. Over the course of the afternoon, four or five different friends spotted Jim with his daughter and made their way over to introduce themselves. These regulars were from all walks of life: the waitress, the guy in a suit, the union worker. There was a predictable pattern in the conversation starting with a warmup funny story about Jim before the tone of conversation shifted. Then every person took the opportunity to recount something that Jim had done for them. They disarmed Jim by couching the tender part in banter, but it felt to Kara like they were all there on the same important errand: to thank Jim Kier. The only way they knew how was to make sure his daughter knew what kind of man her father was. While Jim was at ease, his friends delivered a message that hovered between the spoken words: "Don't let him fool you. Your dad is special."

Jim took the chance that day to tell Kara stories about his youth and as the afternoon waned, he became quiet and said, "My friends are dying. It's the strangest feeling." This truth grew with each breath.

That experience affected Kara and took a long time to fully process. It struck her that the people who came up that day were not the big names in the community. Her dad didn't help people for recognition or payback, he was a true friend to folks who frequented a neighborhood pub. It was a much bigger circle than she had ever realized. That day more than ever before, Kara was star struck over her dad.

After chemo, we asked the doctor if we could still go to our condo at Brentwood Bay and following a recovery, the doctor had no qualms. There in the shower, Jim's beautiful hair was like grass after Round-Up, coming out by the fistful. He had to get it buzzed by Steve's wife Tammy, and for weeks afterward my eye would catch him reaching up to play with it, or reflexively flicking it out of the way like his hair was a phantom limb. Feeling ill is demoralizing enough, but when you look in the mirror and don't recognize yourself, it's hard to put on a brave face. You are reminded every time someone startles at your appearance before catching themselves. It made him as aware as passing a mirror. Maybe more.

One day in the office following a treatment, Annette asked how he was feeling and he said, "Oh, fine. Except this one weird side effect." He half-turned to do something behind his back and then whipped around wearing googly-eyed glasses on springs. They boinged like crazy blood-shot Ping Pong balls and the element of surprise left her in stitches. He repeated the gag all day.

At a follow-up appointment, the oncologist asked Jim about any side effects.

Jim responded, "What you'd expect, but have you ever seen…" then paused and turned to get something from his bag and sprang up with the googly eyes bouncing like rogue electrons, "…anything like thisssssss?"

Throughout the regimen, Jim repeated positive words. He was tough physically, but it eroded his psyche any time he needed help. He had been taking care of himself and others since boyhood, trying to protect everyone within grasp. This was to be a hard lesson. He touched my arm after a sleepless night, "Norma, I'm so sorry you have to take care of me." Words like that were as painful as chemo side effects.

Later he'd remember to say, "Chemo is treatment. We'll beat this." Yes, it's treatment, but it kills good cells as well as the bad, and you live with the unspoken fear that the chemo might not work, or could hasten the end. If Jim ever caught a sad look on me, he'd quote something like, "The body is a miracle and it knows how to heal," or "I'm a fighter."

He fought, yet was also practical enough to schedule additional meetings with our estate attorney, which he justified as something we should do at our age anyway. It was no different than how we had drawn up wills when the children were little. He wanted the details set forth in the clearest, fairest manner. He wanted to avoid family bickering.

His body responded well after a few months and his hair sprouted like little Christmas trees, a good sign. Rebirth and regrowth. It even came in the same. You never know if you'll wind up with different hair altogether, curly where it was straight before or even a different color, but Jim's hair was unchanged. He was unchanged.

We continued like the whole thing had never happened. Summer shined with that feeling where it's hard to even remember what midwinter feels like, impossible to imagine the garden blanketed in white and muffled in stillness.

Kara was living in Oregon at the time, but she and her son stayed with us a lot during those years because she was doing graphic design for a real estate development firm in Park City. It was the perfect fit in an industry where she had roots, but with independence and flexibility. She worked remotely from Oregon, but often stayed with us when she needed to visit headquarters. She also freelanced for our businesses, which kept her involved without being burdened with family politics. As our family's free spirit, working on her own gave her a sense of autonomy.

I noticed that Kara was much like Jim in her ability to connect with clients at all levels in an organization. She treated everyone the same from receptionists and interns to CEOs of big corporations. They reciprocated. Whenever any of the other kids had a tiff with one another, I sensed that they envied Kara's independence and the way she ignored rules that did not suit her. Kara has always been blessed with a sense of who she is and an endearing confidence. She is the same person in all circumstances, true to herself and fiercely loyal to others.

We really enjoyed having her around and got very, very close during that time. She often brought Jim to appointments and insisted on giving me a break that I would otherwise not have taken, shooing me out of the house to get a massage or my nails done.

She would say, "It's cool, Mum, I've got you. I will hang out with Dad. Now you go take care of yourself. And eat something while you're out, will ya?"

While Kara and her son were with us, Jim shined as a grandfather. With the boy's biological father not in the picture, Jim stepped up to fill the role. He and grandson went fishing together and Jim brought that cute little kid along most places he went. Kara would come home from work in Park City and the two would usually be out doing something together.

At the dinner table one evening, Kara's son back-talked her and Jim's commanding voice snapped, "You need to listen to your mother. She is the best friend you will ever have." The boy looked startled by his tone and turned big puppy eyes to his mom in an appeal of sympathy.

She shrugged, "Sorry. This guy is my dad and he is the boss of me. We both have to listen to what he says."

One day when Jim needed a platelet transfusion, he came out wearing his Halloween vampire teeth. "I vant to drink some blood. Ha–ha–ha-ha!"

Leaves fell, and as fall slid into winter of 2004, Jim got sick. Our spirits dampened at the thought of chemo again. You can do it once without flagging, but it's hard to be cheerful knowing exactly what you're in for. He privately admitted, "It's silly, but I don't want to lose my hair a second time."

We started treatments anyway, and on the Saturday before Christmas, Steve's wife Tammy was to come by to buzz his hair. Before that, however, we heard a rap on the kitchen door. Steve and Scott entered and stood there. They both had shaved heads. Jim threw back his head in laughter and they compared noggins. It's hard to put words on the layers of meaning expressed through a single act of solidarity. So much can be said, so much set right in one moment.

He continued treatments through the spring, and as we opened the pool for summer, Jim was getting weaker, not stronger this time.

For Father's Day, the kids and I delivered an energetic little addition to our family: a beautiful longhaired Sheltie Shetland Sheepdog Jim named Boots after a dog he had in boyhood. The kids had read how pets often help ill people recover, and we were ecstatic at having a dog. Before we could keep him, though, he went for several weeks of obedience training, and afterward returned to us the best-behaved dog I've ever known.

That July I wanted to throw Jim a 74th birthday party, but he hated being at the center of attention. The kids suggested throwing me a party also, and we compromised by having one for both of us. So we celebrated a joint birthday party, but truly this year, I wanted it to be about him. It felt like half the town came out to the Country Club—a risk given his immune system. But at this point, the odds are worth it because you become even more aware of how precious your relationships are. You want to savor them and enjoy them every chance you get. You start making bargains with God that if He blesses you with another decade, you'll live every moment to the fullest.

We had music and Jim still had enough stamina for a slow dance together. A packed dance floor kept the mood celebratory throughout. This *wasn't* a funeral. Still, I couldn't suppress thoughts as our guests filed in: *They came while they still can. Nobody wants regrets.*

After that we went in to hear results from a blood count check and the doctor delivered news.

"He has developed leukemia in addition to lymphoma." Jim shrugged it off.

"We'll just keep after the treatments. I'll be fine." It was easy to believe in recovery because Jim had always been so doggone convincing whenever he believed in something himself.

Soon after that, we went to Victoria with Steve and his family. Tammy and the kids went up with us early while Steve and Scott went on their annual fishing trip. Jim wanted to go, but I put my foot down since he was weak and the weather so chilly. There was another change that trip; we had recently sold the Highlander because it was too much work now. We hated to part with it, but always a practical man, Jim faced it.

When the boys came in from their fishing trip, Jim told them, "Tough year. One of the toughest. We had to sell the Highlander and I couldn't go fishing with you guys." It was the first time he ever missed the annual trip.

Even without sailing, it was wonderful to be in Victoria and to spend uninterrupted time with family. After we got back and I unpacked, Jim fell on the stairs and I couldn't get him back up. I called Steve who lived just five minutes away.

Then I dialed the oncologist who said, "Get an ambulance. The cancer is eating his blood and he needs a platelet transfusion." While we were in the hospital, the doctor recommended a special hospital in Houston, so two days after we checked out of our local hospital, I repacked and we were on a flight.

In Houston, he received a treatment, but afterward he had to be admitted into ICU. When I phoned the kids, I could hear shock in their voices, "Intensive care?" Jim's acting had been good.

Around this time, Bonnie and Kimi could see Jim was getting very sick, so they created a new company, Kier Property Management and Real Estate, and took over all the contracts on the properties that we owned. They eventually took over running Kier Corporation.

I had to make a difficult phone call to Kara while Jim was in ICU, "I won't make your graduation. I'm just heartsick about it. Let's make arrangements for Kimi to take my flight." Kara had been working so hard to finish her Master's degree with University of Phoenix, and I was scheduled to fly to Phoenix, Arizona, and attend in person with her.

The day before her graduation, I was pretty blue in Houston. I heard a knock on the door and when I opened it, she stood there in her cap and gown. What a joyful surprise. We had dinner that night at the restaurant hotel (which was adjacent to the hospital). Jim wasn't feeling well, but he mustered the energy because he wanted to be there for Kara.

Kara and I ordered champagne and took pictures in her cap and gown. Other restaurant patrons came up and congratulated us, and we had the loveliest time. Education was such an important value to Jim that it meant so much to see his daughter—the one who had always followed her own beat—earning an advanced degree. All three girls had graduated from college and we were very, very proud of that. Not only was it a wonderful accomplishment, but I could see their confidence grow.

Every few days, another of the children would fly out to see us. We knew the thought without saying the words, *what if this is the last chance?* As difficult as hospital stays are, the urgency to spend individual time and just being together without distraction was a blessing. It could be worse. People lose loved ones to sudden accidents or heart attacks without fully grasping just how much a person means until they are gone. Someone is in your life one day, then poof, gone the next, without a chance to say what is in your heart. As cruel as cancer is, it gives you time.

We had only planned for a short stay in Houston, but it ended up being a month and a half. I had the kids bring me more clothes and an adding machine so I could pay bills from the hotel. Each of them came as often as they could and it wasn't lost on me how they each did the costly trip to be there. The hotel staff got to know us well, and after a rotation of the children coming through, I remember one of them saying, "Just how many children do you have?" My heart was full of gratitude. Five. We had five amazing adult children.

Jim was doing only slightly better after treatments there and overall was weaker than I had ever seen him. I booked a first-class ticket home but was anxious about the flight. What if he got nauseated on the plane? What if he needed to go to the bathroom? There is no room for two people in those little lavatories. We got through the flight without incident and after many prayers for help, I said a few more words of thanks to God.

But he wasn't fine. I wasn't fine. I felt him losing ground and I was getting thinner, too. I canceled all social engagements and clung to him.

I wanted to be right there in case he needed me for anything. I sensed the time we had been given slipping, and I shut my eyes tight. I willed for the clock to stop. Just stop. Freeze it right here. I'll take this. Just don't take him from us.

I thank God for all the times when Kara was there because I needed someone to help me get Jim back up after a fall. She and I began sleeping in sweats so we could head to the hospital in a hurry if a nosebleed started. I would sometimes break down in exhausted, terrified tears. She drove.

We got to know the hospital staff by name, and they knew us, too. Sister Stephanie came by each morning we were in, offering a prayer and encouragement. I wondered how she did it day after day, blessing everyone with such love and cheerfulness in difficult circumstances. She made everyone feel special.

She often greeted us with something like, "Good morning Joe and Helen," and was so loving that it was in the spirit of comic relief that Jim and I would joke with each other after she left.

"What do you think our names will be next time?" Jim would say.

I'd respond, "Maybe Ron and Nancy."

Then Jim would chime in, "I like Judy and Fred."

I never heard anybody speak of Sister Stephanie without them adding something like, "I just adore her," and I felt the same way. She blessed Jim and I so much, and even a laugh together about mixing up our names reminded us who we were.

During this time, we had been building a senior housing project in Salt Lake City developed by the Utah Nonprofit Housing Corporation, which Kier Construction built. When the Executive Director of UNHC, Marion Willey, learned that Jim was ill, he approached our family.

"We want to name the building after Jim."

The idea brought tears to my eyes, both from gratitude and also an ominous feeling. *A memorial*, I thought.

We kept working, and Connie or Marie regularly came to the house to help Jim get things done. I'd fix us all Shepherd's Pie.

One night, Kara and I poured ourselves some wine to drink by the pool while Jim slept. He was in the guest bedroom we had outfitted for us, a convenience with his walker. We talked about her graduation we missed. I felt sad for not being there and sad for any future events her dad might miss. I also shared the news about naming the building after Jim. I should have felt jubilant at her graduation and pleased at the apartment naming—and I was—but I was also spent. I had lost weight and my emotions were threadbare. It was sometimes hard to keep my patience when Jim got short with me, something I was unaccustomed to. He apologized and then we both felt bad.

When he needed help, his eyes held an unspoken apology, and my little heart would break. He told me, "If I don't pull through, I hope you will remarry. I hate the thought of you being alone."

There was also the deepest, scariest idea that I never voiced for its pitiful truth: who would I be without Jim? I was only half of a whole. No, I wasn't even that. Jim was so big to all of us, such an inspiring presence, that I felt a harsh reality. My title was Jim Kier's wife, an extension of him. Why wasn't it me going? I couldn't bear it.

Suddenly I was angry—angry at God for allowing mean people to live into old age but taking a wonderful man who still had so much to give. I knew it wasn't right to ask why, but I wanted to know. It made no sense. I had always believed in a just God, but this didn't add up. I stood up fast, rage boiling over from deep, deep inside and I threw my entire wine glass into the pool. Then I collapsed onto the concrete, sobbing and heaving. Kara put her arms around me until I shook more gently and then quieted. A hazy red sun drooped in the valley below, while summer warmth hung on the ground. Fingers of cooler air now brushed against our skin and the evening descended on us.

The crying had a narcotic effect. I slept hard and awoke to a bright Saturday morning. Jim was having a good day and as he picked his way through a little breakfast, I got up to fill the hummingbird feeders on the deck. I could hear little birds flitting in the trees while a scrub jay squawked for a peanut. The peanut feeders were empty, though, and Jim wouldn't be out in the dewy grass pouring sunflower seeds for the songbirds this week. The birds would have to manage. Then Jim and I enjoyed each other's company on a simple Sunday at home together.

In cancer circles, they talk about the last good days. The beauty and ache is that you never know how many there will be. You don't know if a good day signals recovery, or if you've had the last of the good ones.

You've been so tired, and you're clinging to fantasies that your loved one is on the mend so you hop in, and you enjoy pleasant times with wild abandon. You think it's a rebound. You savor every detail of the weather outside whatever it is, and get carried away in laughter. The days are like enhanced digital pictures, super-saturated with color and sound and the experience of food. You're trying to memorize every detail without letting yourself acknowledge that's what you're doing. You're just enveloped with the childlike giddiness of living in the present.

In September, one of his legs swelled up. The doctor told us that if Jim wanted to keep fighting, he would need surgery. It was risky and there was a chance he might not awake from anesthesia, but Jim was upbeat.

"Absolutely, if this is what it takes."

So we checked into McKay Dee hospital and while I did the waiting game with Scott, we talked with a young man who had his laptop connected to the Internet.

He said, "Have you ever heard of Google Earth? Check this out." We scooted over to his screen and he showed us images of Ogden, zooming in on our very house, a car in the drive.

"That is so cool," I said and added, "What an amazing time. Think of the technology and medical care we have."

When Jim came out of surgery, he was very weak and I did not dare leave his side. Scott brought me a sleeping bag and we tried to get a little rest, but I awoke every time Jim stirred or a machine beeped. Hospitals are not the most restful places. When he came home, we still were back at Ogden Regional every few days for platelet transfusions.

I felt Jim's grasp slip. Gravity was pulling him down a steep embankment and no matter how much I dug in a foothold, I could not hold onto him. I had to watch it happen and there was not a damn thing I could do. Life can be very cruel.

Construction on the apartment complex that would bear Jim's name had gone past deadline—as it always seems to do with these projects—and Jim's health was slipping. We were all on edge wondering if it would be done in time. We wanted him to be honored in person. He had always shirked away from attention, but he said yes this time. Then I got a call from Steve.

He said, "Set a date."

I asked, "Are you sure enough to send invitations?"

He repeated, "It will be done. We can cut the ribbon next week."

We scrambled to confirm availability of dignitaries and to expedite the invitations. Grand Opening and ribbon cutting for the James E. Kier senior apartments would be held November 17th. Jim held on and I felt that we would make it, but part of me feared he might be bluffing, that he'd rally, then while we weren't looking, would slip out the back door before the spotlight could shine in his direction. The night before, I breathed a gigantic sigh that it was really going to happen. I went to get his clothes for the following day, but hit a minor snag. He was so swollen around the middle that his usual sport coats would not fit. I ended up rummaging through his closet and finally found a warm-up suit that looked nice in public. We went to sleep and I exhaled.

Then at 3:30 a.m. his nose started to bleed. Kara was there that night and she drove us to emergency as my heart sank. The likelihood of us making it was nil. They usually had to get platelets in from Salt Lake, which took time. Even then the bleeding might go on for hours. On our way to the hospital, I also remembered that we did not know whether we could get a wheelchair.

The staff saw us coming and went into the drill. I wonder now if the fact that this had become routine was the reason they had the platelets he needed, or maybe it was simple grace. Regardless, that saved hours and gave us a small hope of making it. They began the transfusion but the flow of blood would not stop.

Hours passed. At 7:30 a.m., I called it. "Sweetheart, we won't make a 1 p.m. start."

Part of me was relieved to not have to speak at the open house. It wasn't just my nerves; I did not know if I could get through it without breaking down. As I said those words, Jim's eyes flashed, determined to override my concession of defeat.

"Dammit, Norma, we are going." The bleeding stopped, not even five minutes later.

That was so like Jim. Set an unreasonable goal and then send everyone in a flurry to make it happen. Now we had some logistical hurdles on our hands. A hospital's checkout process is never quick, and we needed to get Jim cleaned up, me dressed, and then leave, about ten minutes ago. The hospital team came together and stayed on the job with singular focus until we were out the door. The next detail was figuring out how to get Jim from the car to inside the event. His walker would take too long and he was weak. Borrowing a wheelchair hadn't panned out.

The corner of Jim's mouth winked into a half-grin, "There's a furniture dolly in the garage. Just strap me in like a fridge."

The nurse laughed, "Just stop, you."

She was already wheeling him toward Steve's truck and said, "We'll just put this chair in the back. You can bring it back afterward."

That was outside hospital policy, and my eyes welled with tears at her trust and generosity. The nurse helped Jim into the passenger seat, making him comfortable with pillows while Steve put the wheelchair into the truck. Then Steve and Scott sped with us to Salt Lake.

I piped up with suggestions on the best route before Steve said, "Mum! I've driven this a time or two before." I shushed my inner backseat driver, but still glanced at my watch every few seconds.

On approach, I spotted the girls waiting out front and saw their relief. The event would happen and our dignitaries would not be kept waiting. We had maybe two minutes to spare. As we pulled up to the curb, I was pleased to see how the building's design put such care toward accessibility for seniors who would live there and it gave us an easy approach inside. My family swarmed Jim's door and now we had so much help it was hard to not to be in the way. We got Jim situated in his borrowed wheelchair and I surveyed his appearance. For the first time, I noticed that the warm-up suit I had chosen out of necessity happened to be the same plum color as the suit I was wearing: a complete coincidence. How lovely that we looked nice together.

As we wheeled into the back, former Governor Norm Bangerter who had been our friend for many years spotted us. Norm gasped. It was an involuntary reaction and when he became aware, he quickly tried to compose himself. He did not want to make it harder on us. I knew, though. Jim had lost his black mane, wearing a cap instead. He was in a wheelchair with cotton in his nose. He looked frail. He was dying.

Norm hurried over and hugged me saying, "Ah Norma, the woman who shares my name! It's wonderful to see you both."

As he shook Jim's hand he said, "Jim, my friend. You deserve this."

They got everyone settled into folding chairs and made space to fit Jim's wheelchair. We were seated beside all five of our strong, independent children. Jim and I both panned their row, our hearts full seeing such handsome adults together. They were dressed in smart suits and everyone looked the part of the professionals they had become.

When the time came for me to walk up front, I mustered strength from someplace way down deep, a place you don't know you even have until you're forced to find it because you want something important. You find it because you want something even more than you want to fall apart. I wanted Jim and everyone to hear my words. And you know what? I got through the entire speech, my voice only wavering once as I caught Jim's eye before I paused, gained composure and continued. When I finished, I looked at Jim. He sat taller in his seat and with more vigor than in a long time. My husband was proud of *me*. I was standing up and he was the one listening.

I had just completed the hardest task of my life: I spoke in front of a room packed with dignitaries—the people Jim respected so much—when what I felt like was collapsing into a heap of sobs and exhaustion. But the timbre in my voice surprised me. I delivered every one of the words that I intended, and I honored James E. Kier, my best friend and the best man I would ever know, and he got to hear the words.

I looked at my children there and they beamed. Now done, the kids motioned toward me to stay up there. Then they wheeled Jim up to join me. He now had a dozen roses on his lap for me. I was very, very touched. The day was for Jim, but he wanted to acknowledge his wife and partner. That was when we all showed emotion.

With the program finished, Jim was flagging now. He had spent all the strength he had, so we regretted that we could not stay for the open house, but had to get Jim home. We were both so tired.

Managing was even more difficult at home now. The following week we got by as best we could. One night I tried making up a bed on the floor so Jim and I could lie together without fear of him falling. It was very comfortable and I thought it a good solution until he woke up confused and asking, "Why aren't we in bed? I want to be in my bed." He was in a lot of pain then, so back into the bed we went, with our son's help.

On Thanksgiving, we savored the day. We all knew—even Jim had accepted by now—that it was to be the last holiday when we would say "everyone." It was the kind of day that you try to memorize, and you hope not to ruin it by being conscious of what is coming. Perhaps the best antidote to that kind of awareness is telling old stories, some that I learned for the first time and cannot be repeated here. When Steve and Scott get going, everybody's rolling. Scott got laughing with his whole body, laughs that rippled out to overtake anyone within a mile. We were laughing so hard we were crying.

As the table quieted, someone asked another question, "Of all the houses we lived in growing up, which was your favorite?"

The kids answered fast, "The cabin." My smile came from a tender place inside.

We cleared the table, and everyone lingered waiting for their individual turn to see their dad when he was awake and not with someone else. It would be a chance to say any words that felt urgent. Jim asked the boys for a promise, "Keep doing the fishing trips."

When Kimi visited him, she held his hand and said, "When I came to work with you, I didn't care what I was doing, if it was sales or politics or toilets. I just wanted to be with you." Then she repeated it, "I wanted to be with you. My whole life I've introduced myself as 'Jim Kier's daughter,' and people are like '*Ahh!* Your name means something, Dad. The thing I'm most proud of, is being your daughter."

Jim asked the kids to take care of me, and especially Kara who had arranged her life to be so available to us in those last years. She promised.

The day ended and later in the weekend we were back in the hospital again. By Sunday night, I would not leave his side. That was the second time for Scott to bring me a sleeping bag so I could stay in the room. The next morning the doctor wanted to speak with us, but we already knew.

"Your body is beginning the process of shutting down. Would you like to remain in the hospital or go home?"

He smiled, "Get me out of here!" Then his wishes, "Take me home."

Before we checked out, the hospital staff gathered round. Many shed tears, and one nurse spoke for the group.

"We see many, many patients, but we can't remember anybody as nice as the two of you." I wondered how difficult it must be for those in that profession to say goodbye to patients again and again. They helped me order a hospital bed for him, and we returned to our home.

I was hesitant to call in hospice because when cousin Sheila's husband was in the last stages of cancer, they shooed her out of the room. I wanted to be near Jim every minute, so I told myself I would stand my ground. I decided to call hospice anyway and my fears were unfounded. Those nurses were just wonderful.

Many friends and family came to see us during that time. I remember a visit from our old friend and colleague. He went in to see Jim and I could hear them laughing as Burrell reminded him that, "you'll always be the Head Fisherman." Burrell thanked Jim for being a mentor and friend. Burrell left the room hanging onto his composure, but he spotted me and broke down.

I hugged him tight, he wiped his eyes, and his voice faltered, "I'm sorry to cry. It's just that Jim Kier had more impact on my life than any other person outside close family. You and Jim *are* family."

Hospice taught me how to care for him so I could be by his side every moment. They told me that Jim would slip into a coma. On Wednesday, the nurse told me he was nearing that point and assured me.

"He will still be able to hear you, so you should talk to him. When you feel the time is right, tell him it's okay for him to go. Tell him you will be okay. He's hanging on for you, Norma."

I knew it. But how could I say something I didn't believe? What drew those words out, out from the same place the words had come at the apartment open house, was that I loved him too much. I did not want him to suffer any more. I wanted him with us, but not like that.

So I willed my tongue to say this, "It is time for you to go see your mother and meet your father. I love you with all my heart and I can't wait to see you again. I will be okay, sweetheart."

At 8:15 on the evening of November 30, 2005, his breathing stopped.

GRIEVING

We called Lindquist Mortuary and two men in dark suits came into our home. They confirmed his time of death and asked if they could proceed. I started to say yes, and then faltered.

"I'm sorry..." my voice sounded like someone else's, someone stronger as I said, "Could you leave him until morning? I need a little more time."

The kids added their support and the men in dark suits said, "Of course, Mrs. Kier. We will return in the morning." It was an act of compassion.

We all lingered in the bedroom with him and when it came time to sleep, the girls wanted to stay with me. So the four of us held each other in a small full-size bed beside Jim's body lying still in the hospital bed. We wept and got a little sleep, that peaceful place of forgetting for a flicker of time.

Sleep felt like hang-gliding far above the world in a few moments of bliss. Then at the moment my eyes opened and saw his body, the toy wings collapsed, sending my body hurtling to the ground. Why didn't I die when I hit? Why didn't I awake from the nightmare on impact? It's because when the one you love dies, being alive is your death, and you awake into the nightmare.

The impact smacked my head, making it hard to grasp what was happening, especially as my daughters slept. My eyes rested on Jim's frame. That couldn't be Jim Kier's body. This cancer-ravaged vessel had once belonged to such a strong man, and he had fought so well for so long, but a tsunami consumes everything. I studied his body more, and now it wasn't just the change in his appearance from the illness that made it feel foreign. Without Jim's gregarious, demanding, absent-minded, and ever-hopeful presence, the motionless structure seemed infinitely smaller than when Jim was in there, even at the end, even in a coma. Jim's life force was bigger than any one body.

At dawn, the girls awoke and we dragged ourselves out into daylight. The men in dark suits returned. They left with my life.

It isn't possible. How can someone be here one morning, and not here the next? Is that why I never faltered in believing that Jim lived on? I simply trusted that deep place inside that knows everything. That place inside told me this: Jim did not evaporate, I simply couldn't see him.

A sensation broke through the fog in my mind. It was the smell of food. Someone was cooking breakfast. Would we still eat without Jim? I could not eat much, but noticed how nice it was that all my children were there around the table. It felt like togetherness.

After breakfast was cleared, each of my children pulled out their phones and the calls began. There were so many people to tell.

"Dad slipped away last night. No, we don't know when the funeral will be, but we'll let you know. No there's nothing you can do, but thank you." Where do all the tears come from? It felt like an endless spring that would never stop gurgling to the surface and streaming out.

With everyone on their phones, I stood in a daze, then my eye spotted movement, a type of ground bird with its family that I had never seen before. We often got quail, jays, and the usual songbirds, but this was different. I retrieved an Audubon Society book and learned that it was a partridge covey, the one and only time I have ever seen one in our yard.

Later that day, someone called out from the window, "There's a bobcat in the back yard!" We ran over in time to see a large bobcat run across the pool patio. A pure white skiff of snow dusted the ground and the feline looked well-fed and with a perfect coat, as though the fur around its face had been blow dried. It bounded toward the six-foot fence and cleared it with no effort. We had never seen a big cat or even tracks in the back yard before because they are elusive and nocturnal. It felt spiritual and I said, "It's Jim."

Frail as I was, I needed to get busy on tasks that had to be done. There was comfort in that involuntary response. Focus on the work at hand, Norma. Get busy. Right now. Stay busy. Don't stop or you'll never get up. A horse lying down is a dying horse.

My mind was slow, though. Such a cataclysmic shift wreaks havoc on the everyday process of thinking. The kids were a great help in making decisions because I felt dazed.

I had postponed making decisions about the funeral until after, but now it was time. We called my friend Pat Poce who had always decorated the back yard for summer parties. A florist knew funerals and he gave good advice. First, select a venue. I really wanted our church, Trinity Presbyterian, feeling comfort in a place we had attended together since being newlyweds. We could hold the viewing there, but were forced to find another space for the main service. We knew we needed somewhere big.

Pat suggested Washington Heights church, which was large enough. When we checked it out, though, their sanctuary had cute decorations up for a Christmas production, and that wouldn't do. We finally decided on Lindquist Mortuary in Layton because its chapel could accommodate.

I spent the next few days making calls for the program. I got in touch with Carrie Maxson of Ogden School District. She had worked with us when we sponsored sending the Ben Lomond High School bag pipers to competition in Scotland earlier, and I asked if they might be available to play at his funeral. She was so gracious and promised them there. The other decisions were a blur. All the while I dreaded getting through the viewing and funeral. How would we summon the courage? We would have to. Jim deserved our best.

When I called Marie, I asked her to speak and she paused for a moment. I understood how difficult it might be, but when she spoke, her voice was steady.

"I understand now. Since Jim passed, words have been forming about Jim's life but it was strange because I'm not family and I kept thinking: *You're not speaking.* Now I understand why."

I also asked Steve, of course, and Bob, Annette, cousin Jimmy Robertson, and Wild Bill Wood to speak. I was pleased when they all agreed.

The children were simply wonderful, coming together during this time without a hint of sibling bickering. They supported each other and me. Without being prompted, they each took turns staying at the house with me. Every morning was the same. My eyes opened and sharp red heat shot through me. I wished it would just burn me up and leave nothing behind. I longed to be wherever Jim was, in a place that knew no suffering.

The kids all came over one afternoon and we pulled out box after box of old photo albums. What a beautiful mess we made, sorting through memories and contemplating which to display at the viewing and funeral. Laughter, stories, and intermittent tears. It was then that I took out my favorite picture of Jim and had Connie make me many copies. I trimmed it into a small portrait, and placed it in my bra next to my heart. This became a permanent part of my daily dress; from then on, I carried Jim with me like that.

The girls took out the yellowed letters from before we were married, tied in a blue ribbon, and displayed them at the viewing and funeral with a sign, "Jim and Norma's love letters."

I still felt Jim with us and I pondered what his experience might be like. Did he have all the answers from all the books now? Did he miss us, too, or could he visit as often as he wanted?

On Tuesday night, we held the viewing and I learned something about times of grief. The love from each visitor envelops you. My body was still in a state of shock, but with each person we loved, each friend who made the time to come, I was touched. That support bolstered my body. Everyone carried me. I was so touched by everyone's kindness, and each time I spotted an old friend, I felt a wave of kinship and memory. People came from everywhere, including a colleague who flew in from Washington just to attend the viewing, then hopped right back onto a red eye flight.

I glanced over at my children standing in Kier solidarity, well-dressed and smart. They represented their father. How blessed I was to have them. Guests kept repeating the same story and I think the kids may have been taken aback by how many variations there were on the theme: People told how Jim had helped them in some way. They said it with a sense of urgency—as if they **had** to tell his children. Someone commented "And these are just the people who knew. Think about how much more Jim did anonymously."

It made the loss—not just ours personally, but for the whole community—feel more acute. The question lingered, "Why was he taken?" All we knew was that we, his family, felt the torch pass to us.

When I awoke the next morning, sun came in through the window, and sleep had done a little repair work on my body. Now I felt a sense of duty to get through the day.

Something I did not expect—and I am sure Jerry Burnett made this happen—was a police escort in front of and behind the hearse. Law enforcement cared a great deal about Jim.

At the funeral, we estimated that over 650 people filled every seat—the family he built through a lifetime of his own loyal friendship overflowed the space. Jim didn't just build things, he built people and they came to say "Thanks, friend." Every pew was crammed to capacity.

There were brief welcome remarks by our pastor. Then out of the silence, a hallowed echo of bagpipes drifted from the back, prickling the hairs on our necks and hundreds of people turned in one motion to see the source of music that stirred primal sorrows. The Ben Lomond High School bagpipers, in full Highland dress, marched in step toward the pulpit playing Amazing Grace and Auld Lang Syne. Marie and Bill Wood sat across the aisle from each other, and in the moment, they recognized the haunting notes of Amazing Grace and locked eyes. The sound transcended words, bringing ancient memories of friendship, and the cycle of death, a reminder that James E. Kier's spirit had joined the ancestors.

First music, then words. Marie and Annette's speeches were beautiful and love-filled, thanking Jim for being a generous pro-woman mentor and friend. He had believed in them, and helped them shine.

Our cousin Jimmy Robertson gave a touching tribute to how much Jim meant to the cousins when they were kids, and how much our family still meant to theirs. He told of Aunt Jean's Kier wall in her home and the many visits we made to them and vice versa.

Each of the kids had helped Steve compile thoughts for his talk, which he delivered beautifully. His words included, in part:

"A wise man said, 'A good example has twice the value of good advice.' That man was Jim Kier…Which of the kids was most like Dad?

We all got a piece. Kimi got his politics. Kara is a free spirit and shared his creativity and love of art. Bonnie was Dad's go-to girl, his right-hand man. She was just like her dad: big business in a small package. Scott got Dad's persistence and problem solving. He also has his sense of humor and laughter. When Scott laughs, everyone joins in. I got his independent nature and his desire to lead. The two of us had many spirited debates. Dad would stomp in the house and say, 'Steve is so damn stubborn. Where does he get it?' Mum would just laugh. Dad guided us with discipline. Just ask my butt. Every one of us got solid work ethic from him and we learned that you have to work for things."

After a lifetime of butting heads, Steve honored his father with admiration.

Bob talked about his old friend, sailing buddy, and partner in mischief. He said he kept waiting for Jim to sit up and say, "How much is this extravagance costing?"

He told so many great stories, although one that impressed me was how when Bob had retired, Jim told him, "You really should get back to work." He took the advice and kept working part-time to stay sharp. Even Bob got choked up.

Wild Bill Wood also spoke. He had softened with age and the pony tail was gone. Now in a suit, he looked like something of a university professor.

He said, "The only person I would do this for is Jim Kier." Always articulate, Bill had everyone in stitches through tears, telling Jim's secrets like how he'd sometimes sign my signature on "unimportant documents like deeds and mortgages." He said that in all their years of doing deals together, it never once interfered with friendship.

I had never seen Jim's fun-loving buddies so tender. Everyone spoke of being part of the Kier family. Jim had built a family that included many, and it would survive even this.

After the service, the pipers led us to the grave site and memorial gardens.

Then it was over. The guests left. I had a fridge full of food, a house full of flowers, and no husband. The kids continued to take turns staying with me, but after a few days I said, "You have been so wonderful. I couldn't have done it without you. But it's time for you to go back to your families. I must learn to do this." My body and soul needed rest.

I didn't let myself lie around much, though. Immediately following the funeral, Connie spent nearly a week with me at the house helping me address over 400 thank-you notes. I hand wrote personal notes to everyone who helped during Jim's illness and for the funeral. I wanted to acknowledge every act of kindness.

We had one more difficult task to get through: picking up Jim's ashes. Steve drove me to get the urn I had chosen, a bronze container in the shape of a book. It was December now and I felt as though I wore gauze when I stepped outside, the cold just seeped right into me. The urn must have weighed 40 pounds and Steve placed it on my lap in the car so as not to topple. It was a block of ice and its weight felt crushing. I couldn't stop little shakes and tears from coming, an endless supply of grief that would never quell.

The next day I got up and went into the office. It's what Kiers and Jessimans do. Marie was there and she confided in me that Jim had asked her to take care of me. I put my hand over her mouth, then told her how years earlier Jim made the same promise to her father. We hugged for a long time.

In later years, I would give my grieving friends one word of advice, "Get back to your routine as quickly as possible. Keep busy and don't allow yourself too much time to feel sorry."

In that spirit, I attempted routine, although Marie was very patient with me because I wasn't good for much. Nobody tells you that your mind shuts down and you walk around like you have a concussion. Still, the body is a miraculous apparatus in the way it gets up and functions— even in a fog—out of some primal will to survive, even while the spirit isn't so sure. My personal trainer, Kim Turner, kept coming three times a week.

The fact that we had so much work to do helped me thaw quicker. Bonnie and Kimi were still in the beginning stages of running the property management business and there were so many details they needed to learn. Kimi had so much going on in her life at the time: two young children, building a house, her husband starting his own business, and learning so many aspects of the job fast.

So many times we wished we could ask Jim. He knew so much and had not been ready to stop working. When the boys transitioned, Jim was there overseeing them until he felt they were ready. They might have resented his micromanagement at the time, but it was a benefit the girls never got. The girls rose to it, though, and learned to swim on their own.

Jim left a few gifts in terms of setting up the business for success. One was to arrange for our longtime friend and consultant, Joe Queenan, to advise us. He is an expert in this business, knowing the nuances of government programs and how to get projects through. Every time we wished we could ask Jim a technical question, we gave Joe a call in Yuma, Arizona, and he often came up and stayed at the house. It is not an exaggeration to say that Joe helped us keep property management alive after Jim's death. He took Jim's place as our mentor, completing that piece of unfinished business for Jim.

One time we especially needed Joe was a few months after Jim passed away. Clinton City put us on notice that due to some technical reasons related to the HUD loan at Country Crossing Cottages, we owed a hefty lump sum. Joe Queenan and Doug Fadel helped us work through hurdles and find means to meet our obligations with integrity. I will be eternally grateful to Joe and Doug.

Jim called Annette a week before he passed and talked to her for some time. At the end of the call he got personal saying, "There is nothing they can do for me so I am going home." He asked her to help the girls with the business and she promised. They were then set up to "ask Annette" whenever they have questions and she was extremely helpful with the success of the girls. You know, after Jim passed, there may have been some nervous employees, but they stayed and I believe are glad they did. Bonnie and Kimi rose to the occasion very fast.

Another gift was that before he passed, Jim asked Jerry Burnett, "Will you check on Norma?"

Jerry dutifully patrolled my house for many years until he asked his own son Troy for three dying requests: don't sell the house, continue the business, and look after the Kiers. Troy has kept these promises and we later named one of our complexes the Jerry Burnett Apartments to thank a faithful friend and honor his legacy.

We spent Christmas at the cabin that year as we always do, and after opening presents, Steve said, "Sit down, Mom."

Then he brought out a heart-shaped pendant in diamonds and rubies since Jim and I share that birthstone. On the back it read, "I will be waiting for you. Love forever, Jim." They also presented me with an audio CD made from a recording of us saying our wedding vows that Jim had made.

I should have known Jim would think of this. For Bonnie's whole life she had been helping Jim get gifts for me. When she was little she would go with him shopping and when she was older, Jim would give her his credit card. Sometimes she and I would go together, sometimes staying in Park City. When we found something I liked, Bonnie would get it on behalf of Jim. Before Jim passed away, he asked her to get some nice Christmas gifts for me.

With Kara living in Oregon, we missed each other more than ever, so I made long trips up there. Her employer told her to take whatever time she needed, so we traveled on the coast together, went shopping, and worked some of the immediate grief out of our system. She took care of me when I was so frail.

I've heard that a time comes when your children become the parent. For me, this became most evident during my grieving. I think this is when the roles most reversed.

The next Christmas, Kara gave each of us a touching gift. She spent weeks going through boxes of family photos and hand-making a uniquely beautiful album for every one of her siblings and me. These books included favorite pictures of Dad and memories specific to that person, embellished with special details. These personalized mementos are treasured by all of us. Turning memories into art helped Kara process her grief while she lived away from the rest of us. It was also an example of how her creative skills have blessed our family and businesses.

For a long time on holidays or our anniversary, Marie brought out a thoughtful gift for me that Jim had pre-bought, mostly jewelry. I wished I could give him something tangible on special occasions, too. All I could give was my devotion. It would have to be enough now.

Another detail was that in Jim's immediate absence, I continued the habit of talking to him each night in my chair next to his. I began listening deep in my heart for answers and guidance. Sometimes before our chat I would listen to the song "Remember When" by Alan Jackson and I danced with Jim's framed picture next to our chairs. It felt like it had been written for Jim and me, filling me with memories of our life. I wept every time.

On occasion, I would awake from a dead-sleep hearing, "Norma. Norma." I would sit straight up in bed and look around for the source, but could see no one.

We planned to spread one-third of Jim's ashes into Brentwood Bay the next summer, on Jim's birthday to be precise. The boys scheduled their annual fishing trip for the same time they would take another portion of his ashes with them before joining us in Victoria. The remaining one-third would wait until someday those ashes would be mixed with mine and placed in the ground by our cemetery marker in Ogden. Then our ashes would be in both of our homes, the United States and Canada.

The months passed, and it was time. Kara, her son and I flew into Seattle and ferried to Vancouver Island. It is always a long day and I was tense by the time we unlocked the townhome, slumped bags onto the floor, and Kara headed downstairs for bed. At the bottom, her bare feet went squish in the carpet. She yelled up at me with an urgency that freezes a mother's blood. It sent me running and I saw her safe at the bottom. Relief.

"What's wrong?" I asked.

She frowned, "There's water down here. A lot of water." I ran down the stairs and a dank smell curled into my nostrils.

We surveyed the basement hoping for some mitigating bright side, something that would allow me to say, "Well, at least…"

But it was bad. Most of the basement had about an inch and a half of standing water, and from the looks of soppy drywall, it had been that way maybe a month. The bases of all the furniture bled in water like capillaries up the wood. I sloshed around another minute or two before realizing this was beyond the two of us. Then we went upstairs to look for more damage. The main floor seemed mostly fine, but in my bedroom I noticed damp carpet next to the outer wall at ground level. It must have come in from there. I suspected a ruptured pipe.

The timing was terrible. Every other trip to Victoria was a small group. Why this time, when the entire family was coming? Where would everyone sleep with the basement unserviceable? I wanted to kick the dresser and sweep knick-knacks onto the mushy floor. I wanted to scream, "Really, God? Us? Now?"

I called the disaster cleanup company, but it took three hours for them to show up. We finally went to sleep in silence.

The next day, I got on the phone with an insurance company as others began arriving. They would come in waves with the boys getting there last after their fishing trip. There was a lot of commotion and tasks to get done including groceries and cooking. Bonnie and I went to the store and as we hefted bags out of the SUV, a two-liter bottle of Ginger Ale rolled free. It bounced onto the corner of my foot and a fierce pain shot up my little toe. How is it that the tiniest digits can make such a big hurt? I hopped around, waiting for the pain in my toe to subside, but it didn't. It throbbed and begged for my attention like a hurt child. I had taken this little piggy for granted.

I yelled out loud in the parking lot, "Why, Lord! Haven't I suffered enough?"

We opened the townhome door and when I smelled the damp basement and felt my throbbing toe, I felt a rush of anger. I tried to put on a cheerful face for everyone, but that night after everyone made beds on the floor, I spiraled into self-pity. Flooded condo. Husband's ashes. Broken heart. Throbbing toe. Family with nowhere to sleep but the floor. Why had I been kicked when I was already down? Was it so much to ask for a good trip? Without Jim, all was not well, and never would be again. My body was stiff in bed and my mind went through a bitter monologue.

Do you know what this feels like? Like I'm 15 again, shy and small without you. I was happy to support you. But I was just support. You were the vision. When you had big dreams, they were mine, too. Now I don't have any. Everyone looked up to you, but now all they have is me, useless and with a broken toe. I'm no figurehead. Not that anyone's asking me to be. They miss you, Jim. But I'm the one who is left. I wish it had been me.

The next day was Jim's birthday, July 11, 2006. I awoke and felt reminded of those occasional years when you can't quite catch the holiday spirit. You decorate for the kids and hope they don't catch on that you're exhausted. But today was the day and we would make something of it.

With my head in these thoughts, the boys rushed through the door like the first spring breeze through an opened window. They reminded me of when, as kids, they used to clomp in for dinner after a day of exploring the foothills, smelling of trail dust and sagebrush. Today they carried the sea breeze in with them, their cheeks flushed rosy from the salty breezes and all remnants of work erased. They hefted coolers of salmon inside, each giving me a big hug.

Steve clutched a videotape and Scott said, "We filmed scattering Dad's ashes on the water. It was just awesome, Mum."

He cracked open the cooler and a beautiful salmon lay on top. He went on, "A few minutes later, I caught this magnificent fish. I'll have him mounted to remind me of Dad."

Then we all gathered at the marina where our former skipper Chris was waiting with his sailboat and one of his friend's. We divided between the two boats and sailed into blue summer skies, far into the beautiful waters of Brentwood Bay. I think there's nowhere better in the whole world for sailing. With the two boats side by side, each of us said a few words then pinched some of Jim's ashes into the deep.

They swirled and spread across the surface and Chris said, "By tomorrow they'll be on the West Coast. Some will be in the water, and some will rest on the continent."

Afterward, I took everyone to an Italian dinner on the Bay. The family crowded into the townhome and they each made a bed on the floor. It was like a slumber party.

As Kara burrowed into her sleeping bag she said, "It's been a long time since I slept on the floor by my brothers." I turned out the light on my children as if they lay on the cabin floor, back when we were all so young.

The Monday after we got home was the first James E. Kier memorial golf tournament. We had been planning it for months and would donate the proceeds. I ran into a snag, though, when I tried to get my golf shoe on. My toe was broken and swollen so I could not get into my golf shoes and Steve bought me a pair of athletic sandals. "You are so good to me," I said. The next day I stood at the ninth hole greeting our guests getting compliments on my sporty shoes.

One of the most difficult tasks was going through Jim's things. His books presented a physical and emotional challenge: there were so many of them. What a life this man had built of bricks and books. The kids got first dibs and I sorted the rest into stacks: keep, give to friends, and donate to the library. I begged his forgiveness for the last category, feeling it would be okay if they went to the library where they might be appreciated. Anything that evoked sentimental memories or that might seem useful went into the save pile. One title caught my eye, *Writing Your Life Story*. Keep. Jim and I kept too busy living life to stop and write about it, but I was blessed with more time.

I went into the office nearly every day and kept running to functions for the grandkids, tennis, and working out with my trainer Kim Turner as we had done for two decades. She has kept me healthy with workouts and advice to stay fit and trim. "Body by Kim," I like to say. Gosh, looking back on it, being sixty all those years ago seems young now. Kim has really become a good friend, helping me stay healthy, advising me on what to eat, and keeping me strong for my age. She knows so much about my life and I am very grateful for her.

One night, Kara and I went into my room and Boots began barking like a maniac at Jim's empty chair by the fireplace where Jim and I always sat together and where Jim would read for hours. We felt the hair on our arms prickle and we looked at each other. This was not like Boots, so Kara sat in the chair to calm him down. We have always wondered what that was.

After Jim's passing, Weber State University asked if I would fill his seat on their National Advisory Council, and I was both nervous and delighted. I also joined the Breakfast Exchange Club of Ogden to get myself out on Thursday mornings.

When they asked me to speak as a new member, I told them how shy I was. Afterward, someone said, "*You*? Shy? Who'd have thought?" I realized it was one of the first professional groups that ever got to know me on my own, not as an extension of Jim. One of my favorite parts was giving service, volunteering in the hot chocolate booth in Christmas

Village each winter to raise money for Shoes for Tots. I've hosted the summer barbeque in my backyard three times.

In 2008, Bonnie and Kimi had the idea of acquiring the Marion Hotel from me and renovating it again. After serving Thanksgiving dinner all those years, and knowing the special love their dad had for it, this property meant a lot to them. With so much new development on 25th Street, they wanted to preserve the Marion's mission for years to come. Kier Property Management had maintained it well since our remodel in 1993, but it was time for a full rehab. This would mean a new round of HUD financing from scratch, working with the City, and bringing together many partners. In short, there are an amazing number of moving parts on a project like this and every detail must fit just so. It was to be the girls' most ambitious development yet, and in terms of complexity would rival anything their dad had done—especially since regulations are more onerous, and HUD backing is harder to get.

Bonnie and Kimi researched options and set their sites on a loan from HUD called a 221(d)(4) loan, which would provide the maximum financing, but it had the most difficult hurdles. To begin with, the rules did not explicitly state that a project like this would qualify. There was no prohibition against it, which they liked to interpret as *possible*. They read everything they could and got advice from any experts they could reach. A definitive answer was not forthcoming. Eventually they wrote Ted Toon, Director of the Office of Multifamily Production in Washington for the U.S. Department of Housing and Urban Development. Then they waited.

November of that year marked three years since losing Jim. At first I felt frozen and stiff, hinged together like a tin man. I was gradually thawing now. At first it wasn't a radiant warmth, but rather like a too-hot bath on icy toes. Now, though, the temperature was reaching an equilibrium and my feet were carrying our purpose forward with new plans.

LEGACY

In the spring of 2009 with Boots lying by me, I picked up a pen and wrote Scotland to complete one of Jim's last requests of me. I was surprised that within just six days, I received a reply from the attorney, Mr. Anderson. He was delighted to hear from me, but also saddened to learn of Jim's passing. I wrote about Jim's inheritance and how he had wanted to return it to Falkirk. Mr. Anderson was touched, but there was a bit of a complication. Hospitals in Scotland are operated by the government and they do not accept private donations, but he would find something to meet Jim's intent.

In a subsequent letter, he presented me with a proposal. There was a private organization named Strathcarron Hospice that operated a beautiful center for the elderly with terminal illnesses and could accept donations. Caring staff and peaceful grounds helped people live out the remainder of their days in private dignity. I thought, *this is the one*. So much of Jim's legacy had to do with housing seniors and we had experienced caring hospice services.

I made plans for our family to present the check in person and invited Jenny and Bob to join us. The three girls were able to go, although this was 2009 and Steve and Scott could not, in good conscience, fly to Europe. The recession was bearing down on the construction industry hard, and subcontractors began going belly-up like fish in a poison pond. Each of the Kier companies trimmed costs to ensure job security for our extended employee family. Although some staff reductions would probably be inevitable, they managed it through attrition, then with the newest hourly. The core family would pull together and hunker down. This storm showed no signs of blowing over soon.

Bonnie and Kimi did the same thing, selling trucks, moving into a smaller warehouse, and cutting costs everywhere they could. Jim had taught them to feed the business first and I was very proud of how disciplined my kids were.

The strategy Steve and Scott had crafted years earlier paid off. They had a good eighteen months of work already in the pipeline. Steve hustled to find new projects and Scott sharpened his pencil. They won many jobs on reputation without a bid process and they sacrificed profit to meet payroll. They also kept subs working. Scott's keen instincts allowed him to price jobs with no margin for error.

These skills had never been more important, and Steve said, "We have a secret weapon: Scott. I have never met a finer estimator than my brother, anywhere." They also found themselves doing work back with their roots: affordable housing.

In this climate, Steve got the kind of call every contractor dreads. A masonry product on a recent job had failed, a big job. He and Scott looked and there was no disputing the problem, but the cause was anybody's guess.

They hired an engineer to get to the bottom of it and the answer came back, "Faulty installation."

Steve processed aloud although he already understood, "So that means?"

The engineer blinked, "It means your sub screwed up."

Steve plopped down at Margo's desk and had her pull the file. It was a small subcontractor that had a relationship with Kier Construction going back a long, long time. Steve put his face in his hands to think, "This will put him under."

Then he sat up, "Kier Construction will not do that. We will figure something out." The script in these situations generally reads something like this: the developer blames the general contractor, the GC blames the sub, and the sub tries to get anyone bigger to pick up the tab. Somebody has to pay, and everyone hopes it will be somebody else. Let the best lawyer win.

They had been through scenarios like this before, so they negotiated with everyone to take a manageable portion of the hit. The manufacturer provided new materials at cost. The developer forfeited profit, and sub provided free labor. Kier Construction carried the sub's financial portion and allowed him to work it off over time. They picked up whatever liability remained. Their dad would have been proud.

We left for Scotland in that economy, which is why Steve and Scott could not get away. Bonnie, Kimi, Kara, Jenny, Bob, and I all arrived in August 2009. Bill Anderson and his wife met us at the hotel pub and we talked about the function and the next day we toured the hospice center. Although it was pouring rain, the grounds and facility were lovely anyway, not at all dreary. The residents seemed well-cared for, socializing in craft rooms and a greenhouse where they potted plants.

At 2:00 we were invited into a room where the current Provost, reporters, our family, Bill Anderson, and others assembled. In the center of the room was a large framed photograph of Thomas Kier and when we spotted it, Kara clasped her hand over her mouth.

"What is it?" I asked.

She said, "That's Steve staring at us." She was right. We had always thought Steve had a lot of Jessiman in his looks, but it was almost eerie to see such strong family resemblance in a photograph a hundred and fifty years old.

The event was more formal than I expected, and thoroughly wonderful. They brought out the Provost's ceremonial robes for me to wear, with a long red velvet cape trimmed with ermine and jewelry belonging to the town for occasions like this. The current Mayor said that while in office, he had not yet had an opportunity to wear the jewelry they placed on me. I was flabbergasted at being dressed up. Throughout the entire ceremony cameras went flash, flash, flash and I felt like queen for a day.

I was expected to speak, and I explained that this would pay tribute to my sweetheart and Jim's great-grandfather, Thomas Kier, because they both set such an example of giving to others. I also told of Jim's accomplishments because I wanted the people of Falkirk to learn of Jim in the same way we learned about Thomas Kier.

I got through the speech and when my knees stopped knocking, I presented the giant show check. It read "To The Strathcarron Hospice in loving memory of Thomas Kier and James Kier." The Falkirk Herald published a color picture of this event.

Next, local historian Ian Scott spoke about Falkirk during the Thomas Kier years. He told everyone how the timing was uncanny because they were preparing to mark the 150th Anniversary of the most important piece of legislation ever passed for the town of Falkirk. As Provost, Thomas Kier had been its principal champion. Mr. Scott was working away on an article that would soon be published in the paper to commemorate the event.

The current Provost presented me with books on the history of Falkirk and a little framed watercolor of the town square during the period when Thomas Kier's grocery was located there. They hosted a reception where we mingled over hors d'oeuvres and had the distinct opportunity to try haggis in little pastries. We got brave and each sunk our teeth in. It did indeed have a memorable flavor and one bite was enough to fulfill the occasion's spirit.

After the ceremony wound down, I asked Bill to recommend a good restaurant and took him, his wife, and son to dinner with us. We had the loveliest meal after which they invited us to their home. The chilly, rainy air outside enhanced the coziness of friends, food, and drink indoors. We basked in one of the nicest days I think I've ever spent. If only Jim had been there in person, although I felt him in spirit. The entire experience felt perfect and I did not come down from the high for a month. I still occasionally correspond with Bill and his wife, and we always exchange Christmas cards.

Kara, Jenny, and Bob and I spent two weeks together in Scotland while the other two girls had to get back to work after about five days.

Upon return, a speaker at Breakfast Exchange talked about Ogden's painted pony project and said they still had some available for businesses to sponsor. I thought, *I want one of those!* So each of the companies sponsored a third and we commissioned Scott's secretary Lori Burlson, who was an artist, to create a design. She named it "Northern Lights," and on the head, she painted two red maple leaves. On the breast there are two Canadian geese to represent Jim and I, overlooking five goslings in a pond. A fox looks at its reflection in the mirror to represent the twins, a mountain lion for Bonnie, an elk for Scott, and a wolf for Steve. It is a nod to Canada during the Pioneer Days festival of the city that adopted us.

I continued our tradition of giving to various causes in the community, especially focusing on helping children. I often attended fundraising galas with the kids and the girls liked to go shopping in my closet for dresses, which made me smile. Every one of my daughters are stunning.

For my 75th birthday in 2010, and for Scott's 50th, the kids threw a big party and choreographed a dance number for me featuring leopard print scarves pilfered from my closet. They sang a funny golf song for Scott. Then we had wine and danced.

On March 11, 2011, another of life's joys happened when Kara remarried to the wonderful Mike Ferguson, a fit and fun man who brought a son and daughter into our family. Kara had a son from a prior relationship and I just adore these grandchildren. Kara has such flair for beauty that she put together quite a party and it was a gorgeous day.

In all, we have been blessed with 20 grandchildren and ten greats (thus far). We have not differentiated between natural children and the ones brought into our family by marriage. They have kept life busy and full with their functions, sleepovers, pool parties, and traveling. We are very involved in each other's lives. Grandchildren often come over to help with jobs I need around the house and although I love spoiling them, Jim and I were always firm with the grandkids just like we were with our own. It is important to teach rules and manners, as well as to dish out love and attention. They make my life rich and full.

Each of my children's spouses deserve credit for bringing unique talents and love into our family. These might seem like little details, but they meant a lot to me. I remember Lora coming to help as my private nurse after I had hernia surgery. Tammy always does the granddaughters' hair for dance tournaments. Mike, Kara's husband, is a great plumber who does great work and installed new faucets in our cabin. Steve Herrick brings me presents for Valentine's Day. Kimi's husband Pat is always there when I need help or a strong shoulder to lean on.

Work is ever a thread that stitches our family life together, and of course sometimes tugged at us. Combined, the companies are approaching $200 million in revenues, with Kier Construction doing $140 million in 2017 from $5 million their first year and have diversified into all types of construction from affordable housing to hospitals, auto dealerships, and manufacturing facilities. They employ about a hundred people, not including subs, and Kier Construction is licensed all over the west.

Kier Management has apartment complexes in many states and they do a wonderful job managing them. The girls purchase and renovate tax-credit projects each year, utilizing complex government programs to improve them for residents. These projects are not for the faint of heart. The Marion Hotel project illustrates what I mean.

For several years straight, Bonnie and Kimi had been working on it. In this, I saw Jim in Bonnie's ability to juggle a hundred details and Kimi in bringing players together. I bought out Key Bank's interest in the property and they secured the necessary tax credits. The girls also landed a commercial financing partner, got a nod from the City—including the Landmarks Commission and Ogden Housing Authority for rental assistance. But a gigantic hurdle remained. The girls still had not received either a confirmation or a denial from HUD about the loan they wanted. Nobody in the country had ever done this before and it was exasperating to not hear back.

In January of 2014 they attended a conference in Washington, D.C., where they skimmed the speaker lineup and circled the name of the director they had written. They went to his presentation and talked with him afterward. They explained the mission of the Marion Hotel and pleaded the need for this type of housing in our community. They reminded him they had sent a letter but had heard nothing back about approval for the loan. He seemed moved by their passion and invited them to write again. After he received their new letter, he signed off on the project within two months, a one-time approval and the first of its type to be converted from a Section 8 Mod-rehab project, the older program Jim did so much work under.

In Mayor Mike Caldwell's first week in office, we invited him to tour the Marion and he shook hands with all the men in the lobby area. His genuineness shined and he has been supportive from the very beginning.

The renovation could now begin in earnest. Architects, designers, and Kier Construction got to work. It was fun for the boys to dig into a project that they had done the first time when they were so much younger. They've earned a great reputation for doing tenant rehab-in-place projects, which are quite challenging because you must mitigate disruption to residents living there during the construction.

In 2016—2 years later—we could finally finish the Marion Hotel project, which had been in the works for a full 7 years. Closing meant a big in-person trip to HUD in Denver after weeks of scrambling.

Bonnie, Kimi, Scott, a representative from the title company, the architect, our attorney Doug Fadel, and I were all heading out on the same flight. I ran out, and as the heavy front door thudded shut, I reached for my keys. My heart sank as I realized they were on the kitchen counter. My spare was in the hands of a painter and my kids were already on their way to the airport. I made frantic phone calls including to B.R.B. Patrol but they were unable to get in. Then I called my secretary Marie. She is always so competent and she booked me on the next flight to Denver.

As I waited for a locksmith, I kicked myself for being so careless. I missed Jim. I missed having someone to help, someone with another set of keys, someone to wait with me on the front porch, and someone to make me laugh about it. I felt really alone.

I made my flight to Denver and a taxi delivered me to the historic Brown Palace Hotel where Jim had stayed when he closed big deals. A little before 9 a.m. we assembled in the marble and mahogany lobby and a mood lingered with us in this elegant, masculine hall.

No time to dawdle, though. I glanced at my watch and Doug Fadel approached with a banker's box perched atop a suitcase, with all the files carefully labeled. He cracked the lid open to show Bonnie the paper evidence of all their hard work and said, "Everything is ready now."

He began walking and I said, "Is that secure?" He assured me, and we strode outside into a crisp Denver downtown.

Our heels clicked along the sidewalk and then the rollers hit a crack. The banker's box toppled and its contents took flight like doves at a wedding. We scrambled after our little birds, our feet stomping some onto the sidewalk and our hands catching others. I could almost hear Jim's uproarious laughter from the other side. One for old time's sake.

The HUD building loomed in front of us with mirrored windows on every other floor reflecting the high-altitude sun. Its clean lines and horizontal stripes of alternating glass and brushed metal made it not un-pleasing. It was a functional skyscraper, and not ugly like many Federal buildings, striking a balance of attractive design without being ostenta-tious. Our meeting started on the 25th floor and we still had to get through a badging process.

Once in, we met up with a cadre of HUD people, lawyers, lenders, title folks, and our contingent. We worked in a conference room big enough for the United Nations and mountains of paperwork. Now we began the process of paging through each date, figure, and line. Then the finals had to be produced, reviewed again, and signed. We needed a green light by 3:00, and final funding transmitted by 3:30.

Midmorning, an HUD attorney spoke up, "Oh no. There's a num-ber off by $87 here."

The room's mood shifted from metered efficiency to mild panic. Bonnie and Kimi huddled and said, "For $87 let us just give you the money now."

They knew, though, that it could have been $8,700 or $0.87. An er-ror in any amount was a problem and even a minor revision meant up-dating many documents. HUD staff bustled in and out with a look of permanent worry on their faces.

Lunchtime passed without a pause. Around 2:00 nobody had eaten and personalities got impatient, so the girls and I ran down to the lobby's Starbucks for trays of drinks. It helped.

The clock ticked 2:30, which meant we had less than a half hour for the final nod, and less than an hour to transmit funds. We paced.

We still had not seen a final set of documents by 2:45, then 2:50, and at 2:55 someone brought in a massive stack. That was the "yes" we needed, but everything still had to be signed, notarized, and sent back east. The marathon became a sprint and we lined up with pens in hand. Sign and slide to the next person in line. Repeat. "You missed this date," and so on. 3:05, 3:15, 3:20. At exactly 3:29—and that is not an exagger-ation—the last signature was transmitted. We had sixty seconds to spare. It felt like the whole city let out a great sigh, and we erupted into cheers. I did a victory boogie. I felt Jim saying, "Well done, team."

At 4:00, the seven of us staggered down to street level, our veins coursing with a potent cocktail of elation, low blood sugar, and caffeine.

We went to an early celebration supper where the wine left us laughing and finally coming down.

After all these years, you'd think I would expect the rush that the last signature brings. Then again, this one was different. We had done this on our own. Kimi looked at me with tears welling in her eyes. She said, "Dad taught us well."

On our way to the airport, I craved a warm bath and soft bed, but we still had a flight and drive home. I nodded off, resting my head on Bonnie's shoulder. Before falling onto the pillow about midnight, I sat in my chair beside Jim's and took a minute to tell him about our day. I ended with, "But you already know. I felt you there."

I slept in and lounged the next day, but sprang out of bed the next morning with a huge 80th birthday party and a houseful of guests arriving in a month. There were landscaping projects to be done, furniture on order, and a whole list of other details.

The following week we held a memorial dinner in honor of Sean Herrick, Bonnie's adult stepson who had been killed in an automobile fire in July a year earlier. That had been an incredibly heart-wrenching yet poignant time for the whole family. The Marion Hotel would now be renamed as the Sean Herrick Apartments, partly to acknowledge that each year on Thanksgiving Eve he went down with us to serve Thanksgiving dinner. After we began this tradition in 1993, we never missed it and Sean always gave of himself there.

MEMORIAL WALL PLAQUE FOR
SEAN HERRICK

The story of Sean Herrick's life did not end with a tragic fire, but is completed in a message of hope. This is a story of grace.

If eyes are windows to the soul, then Sean's sparkled with a deep compassion he earned from many private burdens. He suffered from a painful physical disability, spent months in hospitals, and was diagnosed with bipolar disorder. Mental health became intertwined with the chains of addiction. Perhaps his most difficult challenge was feeling unworthy. Those beautiful eyes saw only the good in others, while finding too much fault in himself.

Yet he was a remarkable person, blessing everyone he met. Sean served on many mission trips to Mexico and also loved serving Thanksgiving dinner to residents of this building, which is one reason it now bears his name. He embodied humility and related to anyone who felt judged. He was a hungry reader, an inquisitive seeker, and the kind of friend who stood up for people when they weren't around.

In the weeks before the accident, something uncanny happened as a change washed over Sean. He felt unbound by addiction and was completely sober. He cast off his leg brace and went wakeboarding. He talked about intense feelings of love toward all people, and noticed exquisite beauty in the natural world. He journaled about finally understanding the meaning of grace. At last he felt his own worth, and everyone sensed it. Sean was going to be okay.

Then on an otherwise ordinary day: a vehicle glitch, a tragic fluke, and hours later Sean was free.

Sean Herrick is greatly missed but his brief life shines as an example of God's great love.

FINDING MY VOICE

———————◼———————

The following month bubbled with party preparations. After Jim's passing, I had closed the door to his home office and kept much of it untouched. Now I wanted to spruce it up into an inviting room where we would enjoy spending time, but kept putting it off.

I paused to think about how it had been nearly ten years. Could that really be? We had survived and I felt like a very different person than before he had passed. Shortly after he was gone, I attended a meeting and offered my thoughts. One of the male colleagues said, "I don't think I've ever heard you speak up."

Now I was comfortable in my role as the matriarch. I was expected to represent the family at charitable functions and Steve had begun telling me "no" when I called him to speak. He said, "People want to hear from *you*."

On a rare occasion, I even intervened when the kids were not getting along. Once when I set up a meeting to clear the air, I told Steve, "Don't make me bring my chair," referring to the time he was a kid and I clobbered him with one.

Marie caught wind of me saying that and laughed, "She might not have much weight, but she can throw it."

I still traveled every chance I got, and whenever I bought something nice on vacation, I touched it and said, "Thanks, hon." Jim left me the means to enjoy my life now. I made sure to visit Kara and her family several times a year. Technology is a wonderful way to stay in touch and no matter where she lives, we stay close by phone, text, or email. Kara has always had a sixth sense about what is going on with her loved ones, especially Kimi. She reaches out if she feels anything amiss. Being so far away will never get easy for her and I remember what it is to cry at the end of a call or visit.

My doctor sometimes lectures me about being more careful. "Your mind is young, but your body really is 80."

After one of these lectures, I told my family, "When the time comes, I don't want a funeral. Throw a life celebration and my requirements are these: Everyone must wear leopard print and there will be dancing, chocolate, and wine."

I never have become used to attending functions or a Jazz game by myself, so I often ask Tom Hart from our office to go with me. He is a handsome, divorced man in his 50s and I am always so grateful when he says yes. He's nice about it, saying, "I would be delighted to go with you." There may have been a man or two interested in more, but from the time I was fifteen, I never wanted anyone but Jim.

We truly were Canada geese. They raise their young together and stay by the other's side when one becomes injured or dies. They are social creatures with a big flock around them, but if an older goose loses a partner, they often never mate again.

Now after ten years, I opened the doors to Jim's home office and finally felt ready to tackle it. I had the cabinets refurbished in a lighter wood, the walls painted, and new furniture with Scottish pillows. I brought out Jim's family heirlooms and displayed them in a beautiful cabinet, and arranged his favorite books.

The week of my actual birthday I kept even busier than usual with the annual Breakfast Exchange barbecue one evening and I also hosted our tennis group's annual pool party at the house. On Thursday night, my daughters took me to see the second *Magic Mike* movie, saying "You're the sexiest 40-year-old we know." We laughed and had a great time.

Friday morning was my actual birthday and I played tennis. My instructor said, "I need to get you into the senior tournament in St. George. You will run everybody else out." Steve Herrick surprised me by bringing flowers to the court afterward, a touching and thoughtful gesture. After that, my son Steve and I had coffee and a lovely chat.

That afternoon when I returned home, the front porch was bursting with the biggest rose arrangement I had ever seen; the kids bought me

80 roses in all colors. The card made me cry. Later that night, Bonnie and Scott came over with their families for a barbecue. I savored every hug and phone call. I had Happy Birthday sung to me from Eastern Canada, Western Canada, by local friends, and in Chinese by my granddaughters who are in a Chinese immersion program.

On Sunday, I supplied the flowers at Trinity Presbyterian and had the card read, "Thank you Lord, for a blessed 80 years." My heart felt as full as that arrangement of roses, each year like a temporal flower, a gift.

As Pastor Monica made the week's announcements, she said, "I think this is the first time the Lord has ever received flowers at this address."

It's not like you are different following a birthday, but zero birthdays do call you to reflect, and 80 carries a special weight. The thought exists but nobody says, "At this age, you never know." I've had to bid a farewell to high school chums and dear family at funerals and everyone in the cohort thinks, "Which of us will be next?"

I also remembered how when the children were little, I thought I couldn't possibly love them more. As adults, they had become the most wonderful parents and now I have more fun with my grown children than anyone else. Our five children—with their unique gifts—have grown the Kier family of companies beyond anything Jim and I could have done alone.

On the days before the party, friends came from all over. Nine people stayed at the house: Jenny and Bob, our friend Betty Dooher who had thrown me the going away party in Britannia, her niece Theresa from Denver, my sister Barb and her boyfriend Mel, Kara, her husband and kids, my brother Jon, and our consultant Joe Queenan and Rhonda from Yuma, Arizona. Some were there for the entire week, which was wonderful.

Betty Dooher said, "This is my kitchen now. Go enjoy yourself." She kept everyone fed and helped clean up after. Later I sent flowers to thank her in a small way.

I had ordered a new dress to wear, a long Hawaiian print gown with a slit up the side. It looked too small, but then I noticed the fabric had some give, almost like a bathing suit. To my delight, it was not constrict-ing. I smiled to myself that I was going braless to my 80th birthday party. Jim would approve, though.

Tropical flowers brightened every corner of the Country Club. My daughters took turns standing beside me, putting leis on guests and mak-ing sure everyone signed the big picture they had matted. A luscious cake looked like a bamboo hut with edible flowers cascading down and a hula girl on top. A deejay played music and my hips did a little wiggle bug in place.

I beamed with each new guest and greeted everyone with delight. Chris Zimmerman said, "I have to tell you, 33-years ago tonight, we had our wedding reception right here. We just came from our granddaugh-ter's first birthday party, and now are here for your 80th. It feels like we're celebrating all the joys of life tonight."

Midway through the party, my sister Barb spotted a couch in the lobby and said, "Norma has kept us so busy, I'd like to lie down right there."

Betty Dooher laughed and said, "I will join you."

A digital recorder circulated so guests could share memories for this book. Someone remarked, "Jim found whatever he needed from a book. How fitting that there will be a book about Jim, sharing what he learned."

After, the deejay fired up and I stood in back. Kimi nudged Scott in the same way Jim used to do, "For Pete's sake, will somebody dance with our mother?"

Someone said, "Canadians know how to throw a party!"

The evening wound down in a way that makes people tender and my brother Jon asked me to dance. He said, "Norma, I have cherished dancing with you for the last 55 years." I loved him and my sister Barb more than I could say.

After the party, I closed the blinds and kissed my two fingers on Jim's picture, then sat in the chair by his. "Wasn't that the most marvelous party? I felt you there, and I hope you enjoyed it as much as I did. Thank you, Jim, for this wonderful life. Happy birthday."

Then everyone left. After the last plane ascended into the sky, I returned home to a big, silent house.

It felt empty now after being on a high. I was tired. I slumped onto the carpet and I felt ashamed of self-pity, but a wave of grief came on. It was like being alone again after the funeral and the wound needed a little fresh care.

In November, the tenth anniversary of Jim's passing was a solemn day and I spent time with the kids.

Then in mid-December I received a telephone call, "This is Chuck Leonhardt, Chamber President." He continued. "You and Jim were nominated and selected as this year's recipients of the Chamber's Wall of Fame Award. It recognizes a lifetime of service to our community. Will you accept?" I was stunned, but must have said yes. Then he continued, "The dinner is February 5th. You will have a few minutes to speak." Then the blood drained from my face.

Steve and my other children were among the first to call. I said, "I guess I had better look for a dress." Isn't it always about the dress?

I went to work on the speech as I wanted to get the words right. How would I get through it? I re-worked it and said the words aloud in Jim's study, which gave me strength.

In a catalog, I eyed a floor-length gown with long sheer sleeves in champagne lace. It had a black lining that looked like a slip underneath. It might work: fitted and a hint of sexy, but still appropriate. When I opened the box, it fit perfectly except, of course, for the length.

I told the boys, "If I faint, it's your job to dash up and finish reading my speech. *Then* you can pick me up off the floor."

When Tom Hart arrived that night to pick me up, I said, "I think we've known each other long enough that I can ask a real favor. Would you zip me up?" I had tried and tried to reach around, but couldn't quite get it. We both laughed.

Friends buzzed to congratulate our family and I must have hugged hundreds of people that night. We had two tables, Kier Property Management at one and Kier Construction got another.

Earlier in the week I said to Kevin Ireland at the Chamber, "You might have to get something for me to stand on." He assured me it would be fine, but when I saw the tall podium, I had doubts. Then I realized that I had not asked anyone to stand behind me in case I fainted. Then I thought, *Jim will do that tonight. He will stand beside me.* I had done that for him, and now he would give me courage. The Lord would be there, too.

I felt joyful all evening. The program had our picture and highlights with this final note:

"Norma celebrated her 80th birthday in July. November marked the tenth anniversary of Jim's passing. This coming September would be their 60th wedding anniversary and 2016 is 55 years in business for the Kier family of companies."

As dinner was served, however, I got more anxious. It's not very nice to make the main recipient speak last, wringing their hands the whole time. There was a lively murmur as many tables half listened to the presentations and half socialized. That is the nature of an evening like this. I thought to myself: *If people are talking, it won't matter how I do.* Bonnie nudged me, "Mum, eat something." But I could not touch it.

The Weber State University Choir came up and I hoped the music would have a calming effect. Instead of a hymn, they sang a snappy arrangement of the ridiculous song "Short People" and the two Kier tables cracked up laughing. They must have known we were coming. Laughter is a wonderful tension breaker and the knot loosened. Maybe comic relief was a bit of grace.

Then my legs responded with muscle memory, pushing me up the steps, across the stage, and to the podium. I peered out and joked that they chose the song as a special welcome for me and I made a spontaneous comment, "My grandmother used to say dynamite comes in small packages."

Then I felt more at ease than for any other speech in my life. With six hundred pairs of eyes in a vast conference center, I could hardly believe it. The rehearsed words came out and I included brief anecdotes about our children that I had given myself permission to skip. I felt encouragement from every corner of the room. They were generously giving their love. The room was silent, which might have made me nervous, but I understood that they wanted to hear. I spoke loud enough that they could. I said this:

"People often comment, 'How do you all work together? If I worked with my family, we'd kill each other!' The truth is, we didn't always get along. Jim and I had a great marriage, but we would sometimes go the rounds and we each got to have our say. Also, when you make a lifetime commitment, you keep working it out, no matter how many times it takes. Our children have made a lifetime commitment to each other. They are business partners and best friends. *Most of the time.*"

My voice broke ever so slightly at one part:

"Jim was an amazing man and he made me a very happy woman. We were a great team. He was a loving father who dished out discipline when needed. He had a brilliant mind and knew where housing needs of people were headed. And maybe it sounds quaint, but from the time I was fifteen, Jim Kier was my hero and still is. It was quite a ride, and we'd do it all over again."

Then the tempo picked up again and my voice regained strength.

"In closing, I want to thank the Chamber for this awesome honor and each of you for your friendship. I will treasure this evening for the rest of my life. I still feel like that shy girl from Canada who married her high school sweetheart. We had nothing but dreams, adventure, and each other. From the bottom of my heart, thank you."

Then it was over and people stood. I've had many dreams come true, but a standing ovation by six hundred people is one I could never have imagined. *Look, Jim. This is for us.*

At home, the hum of energy began to wane. Heels came off as Boots greeted me inside. He was slowing down now, but always still excited to see me. I went downstairs barefoot, ready to peel off the dress and collapse. Except I couldn't.

I tried reaching my arms around, twisting one way, then angling my arm over. Nothing doing. I wondered if I might find some pliers to free myself, then imaged sleeping in it bound like a snake. No, I had to get out of that thing. A few minutes later I was on Kimi's doorstep knocking. When she saw me, her face flashed with panic.

"I'm alright, everything is okay. It's just I can't get out of this dress." It was like spontaneous combustion first with her face and then her body overtaken with laughter. She'd get to the zipper, but we first had to work out the laughing fits. She unzipped my gown and sent me off with a hug.

Unbound, I returned home, slipped on a pretty nightie, and held Jim's picture to my chest.

We ended the evening in a private slow dance together.

Remember When?

A LOVE LETTER FOUND

The week after we finished last drafts of this book and met with the printer, I was in intensive care after a heart attack and stroke. I had been feeling terrific earlier in the year going on a once-in-a-lifetime African safari, playing tennis two times a week and working out with a personal trainer. Genetics, however, caught up to me. My siblings suffer from the same issues and my dad passed from a heart attack far too young.

Doctors tell me I can live like this if I cut my activity level by half, and I admit I was feeling blue about having to give up tennis.

At that exact time Bonnie's secretary Tracy found a spiral-bound notebook in Jim's credenza lying there, untouched since his passing.

The pages were pre-printed with the label "Project Planning Notes," and on the numbered lines below, Jim had penned a letter. He wrote a special note to each member of our family beginning with these words:

> *Since this could be my last words, I wanted everyone to know that I could not have asked for a better wife and children and I am very proud of all of you, including all our grandchildren. Norma, a special note to you - for all the years you have stood by me. What a lucky man. I could not have accomplished what we have done without your help or love. I will love you always...*

I like to think that the timing of finding this letter was not a coincidence.

ABOUT THE AUTHORS

Norma Kier: In 1957, Canadian newly-weds Jim and Norma Kier moved to Ogden with just $100 in their pockets. Ogden soon became home and the two began saving their pennies to start Kier Construction, which they founded in 1961. For the next decade they ran the business from various homes, living on "scrambled eggs and beans" to invest in their fledgling company. During the coming years, Jim and Norma had five children, who they brought into the business since day one: Steve, Scott, Bonnie, and twins Kara and Kimi. Together, they built countless landmarks in Ogden. The Kiers never forgot how it feels to struggle and have given back at every opportunity—especially to causes benefitting children and those less fortunate. In 2015, Norma accepted the Ogden-Weber Chamber's *Wall of Fame* award recognizing the lifetime contribution that she and Jim have made to the community.

Rhonda Lauritzen is a professional biographer and author on telling personal stories. Before founding Evalogue.Life, she served as a technical College Vice President. However, it was working in the family business—ultimately as CEO—that inspired her first book, *Every Essential Element.* That family business memoir is told in her mother's voice. Lauritzen loves learning and teaching the craft of story, and lives with her husband and daughter in an 1890 Victorian they restored. Their home is in Ogden, Utah.